COOK NOW, DINE LATER

COOK NOW, DINE LATER

Catherine Althaus
and
Peter ffrench-Hodges

FABER & FABER LTD
3 Queen Square
London

First published in 1969
by Faber and Faber Limited
3 Queen Square London WC1
This edition published 1972
Reprinted 1973 and 1976
Printed in Great Britain by
Jarrold and Sons Ltd, Norwich
All rights reserved

ISBN 0 571 09895 9 (Faber Paperbacks)
ISBN 0 571 08815 5 (hard bound edition)

CONTENTS

INTRODUCTION

Most people who like to cook good food have other occupations. This book is for them. Here is the solution to the panicky homecoming laden with shopping, the frenzy in the kitchen, the front-door bell earlier than expected, guests being bundled into chairs with the gin bottle, so that when, hours later, the cook announces dinner, the gin bottle is empty and nobody cares any more about food.

Unless one is extremely well organized, it is very difficult to cook and look after one's guests on the same evening. This book turns back the kitchen clock; dispels panic by giving stage by stage directions and details of the preparation which should be done before cooking starts. The good cook of today is transformed into the confident host or hostess of tomorrow.

Cook Now, *Dine Later* has two main themes. The principal one is that all dishes can be prepared in advance, either the day before or, in certain cases, the hour before, thus leaving virtually nothing to do on the evening but entertain your guests until it is time to go out to the kitchen to dish up. All the dishes, except where the recipe says 'serve immediately', will keep well in a low oven, if your guests are late.

Secondly, in order that cooks should know just how good their food is, they should have tried it out before they present it to their guests. This is the idea behind our having given the quantities for two and for six people, plus the fact that we have wanted to help the many people who like to produce something different every night and are tired of adapting large quantity recipes. All the figures in brackets in the recipes refer to the quantities for six people.

The book is divided into three principal sections: Beginnings, Mains and Afters. These sections are sub-divided according to the basic ingredient.

7

Following the main part of the book are four appendices.

Appendix I gives details for making such things as pastry, mayonnaise, stock and white sauce, which are referred to throughout the book and for which no recipes are given at the time.

Appendix II is devoted to vegetables and potatoes that can be cooked and kept in the oven without harm, and to salads, with particular emphasis on more unusual winter salads.

Appendix III is entitled SUPPERS AT SHORT NOTICE. This section was devised for those occasions when you, or a member of your family, rashly invite friends to a meal without much thought for your larder, and probably after the shops have closed. We have suggested a list of 'Storecupboard Standbys' from which you can make a choice of thirty-two dishes. The recipes for some of these dishes appear earlier in the book, and others are given in full in this section. None of these dishes requires more than an hour's notice and most take well under an hour.

Appendix IV gives a selection of three complete menu suggestions for each month of the year, utilizing foods as they are in season. We have done this because we have found whilst writing this book that friends have asked us not so much 'how shall I cook it?', but 'what shall I cook?'

GENERAL NOTES ON THE USE OF THIS BOOK

1. Since this book is devoted to recipes for dishes which can be made in advance, the cooling and reheating of food is involved, and the following important points emerge from this:

   (i) It is very important to let food cool completely before putting it in the refrigerator.

   (ii) It is important to remember when food is taken out of the refrigerator that unless you are using metal or specially strengthened glass or porcelain casseroles, you should allow the container to reach room temperature before putting it in a hot oven, otherwise it may crack.

   (iii) When reheating meat or fish, it should first be brought up to bubbling point and left there for 10 minutes. This is achieved by putting the dish in a very moderate oven for 1 hour, or into a hot one until this point is reached, depending on the recipe. You can, of course, if you are using the metal or strengthened glass or porcelain dishes, bring the food quickly to boiling point on top of the stove before your guests arrive, and then put the dish into a very low oven to keep warm.

2. *Liquid Quantities*

   Throughout this book liquids have been measured in fractions of a pint, spoonfuls, glasses or cups. To give an indication of the size and capacity of the utensils we used, a table is given below:

   2 teaspoons   = 1 dessertspoon
   3 teaspoons   = 1 tablespoon
   5 tablespoons = 1 sherry glass
   10 tablespoons = 1 wine glass, 1 cup or 2 sherry glasses

3. *Dry Quantities*

As an approximate guide to the dry quantities used in this book the following table is given:

$\frac{1}{2}$ oz. flour = 1 level tablespoon
1 oz. flour = 1 heaped tablespoon
1 oz. sugar = 1 level tablespoon
$\frac{1}{2}$ oz. butter = 1 level tablespoon

All spoon measures given in the recipes are rounded unless specifically stated otherwise.

4. *Stock*

In the recipes calling for stock you can substitute stock made up with either a chicken or meat cube, and water, except in the instances where a court bouillon is required.

5. *Flour*

All the recipes in which flour is mentioned are made with plain flour.

6. *Frozen Pastry*

No mention of frozen pastry has been made in the text, but as this is now in such general use it should perhaps be mentioned as a substitute in cases of emergency. Remember that time must be allowed for it to unfreeze.

7. *Herbs*

Fresh herbs are naturally better than the dried version, but on account of the difficulty in obtaining fresh ones, dried ones can always be substituted in the recipes. There is, however, one exception to this rule, we always use fresh parsley. It should be noted that smaller quantities of fresh herbs are needed as they have a more pungent flavour before they are dried.

TABLE OF COMPARATIVE OVEN TEMPERATURES

				Electricity	Gas
Very Slow	.	.	.	250–270 degrees	Regulo ½–1
Slow	.	.	.	300–325 degrees	Regulo 1–2
Very Moderate	.	.		325–350 degrees	Regulo 3
Moderate	.	.	.	350–375 degrees	Regulo 4–5
Moderately Hot	.	.		375–425 degrees	Regulo 6–7
Hot	.	.	.	425–475 degrees	Regulo 7
Very Hot	.	.	.	475–500 degrees	Regulo 8–9

Beginnings

The Day Before

Egg Mousse

2 eggs	(6)
¼ small tin consommé	(¾)
1 dessertspoon salad cream	(2)
1 tablespoon double cream	(3)
1 teaspoon lemon juice	(3)
seasoning	

Preparation

Hard boil the eggs and allow to cool.

Action

1. Peel and finely chop the hard-boiled eggs, and if you have an electric blender put the eggs in it with the consommé and mix until smooth. If not, just mash the eggs as finely as you can and stir in the consommé.

2. To the eggs and consommé add the salad cream (not home-made mayonnaise on this occasion), the cream and lemon juice to taste. Season with freshly ground black pepper.

3. Pour the mousse into individual dishes and chill in the refrigerator until required.

Next Day

Garnish with chopped iced consommé, or with flower patterns made with the white of a hard-boiled egg, using the sieved egg yolk for the stamens and thin slices of cucumber skin for the stems and leaves.

The Day Before

Red and White Eggs

2 eggs	(6)
2 tomatoes	(6)
1 tablespoon grated mild English cheese	(3)
1 dessertspoon fresh white breadcrumbs	(3)
1 teaspoon sugar	(3)
½ oz. butter	(1)
1 teaspoon flour	(2)
⅛ pint chicken stock (Appendix I)	(¼)
seasoning	

Preparation

Hard boil the eggs and slice. Skin and slice the tomatoes. Grate the cheese finely. Make breadcrumbs.

Action

1. Make a sauce with the butter, flour and stock. (Appendix I)

2. Butter 2 (6) ramikin dishes and place in them alternate layers of egg, seasoning, tomato and sugar until all the egg and tomato are used up.

3. Pour the sauce over the egg and tomato and sprinkle on the breadcrumbs and grated cheese. Chill overnight in the refrigerator.

Next Day

Place little dabs of butter on top of each dish and put them in a hot oven for 10 minutes.

The Day Before

Egg Cutlets

See 'Mains' section, p. 65.

The Day Before

Turtle Eggs

2 eggs	(6)
½ small tin real turtle soup	(1 medium)
½ teaspoon grated Parmesan cheese	(1½)

Preparation

Nil.

Action

1. Heat some water in a large frying pan, so that you could stand ramikin dishes in it and the water would come half way up the sides.

2. At the same time heat the soup in a separate saucepan.

3. When the soup is hot, but not boiling, pour it into the ramikin dishes so that it comes two-thirds of the way up, then break an egg into each dish.

4. Stand the ramikins in the boiling water and cook until the egg whites go white, but the yolk is still soft (approximately 2 minutes).

5. Remove the ramikins from the boiling water and cool. Store them in the refrigerator until you are ready to eat, otherwise instead of being jellied, the turtle soup will go liquid again.

Next Day

At the point of service sprinkle a little Parmesan cheese on each dish.

The Day Before

Bacon Mushroom Egg and Onion Flan

2 rashers streaky bacon	(6)
2 flat mushrooms	(2 oz.)
½ small onion	(1 medium)
1 egg yolk	(3)
1 egg white	(1 large or 2 small)
3 tablespoons double cream	(¼ pint)
seasoning	
4½ oz. short crust pastry	(8)

Preparation

Wash and finely chop the mushrooms. Peel and finely chop the onion. Cut the rind off the bacon and cut the rashers into strips about ½ in. wide. Separate the egg yolk(s) and white(s).

Action

1. Make the pastry (Appendix I), roll out and line a 5–6 in. (8–9 in.) flan case. Prick the bottom of the pastry all over with a fork and in the middle lay a sheet of greased paper or foil on which you should put a handful of uncooked rice or dried beans to stop the pastry rising. Bake in a moderately hot oven for 15 minutes, or until the pastry has set, but without browning it.

2. While the flan case is cooking, put the pieces of bacon in a frying pan over a low heat, and cook them until the fat begins to run out, remove them from the pan, then lightly sauté the chopped mushrooms and onions in the resulting bacon fat.

3. Lightly beat the egg white and yolk(s) and mix with the double cream. Stir in the mushrooms and onions and season well.

4. When the flan case is ready remove from the oven and take out the rice and foil. Allow to cool.

5. When the pastry is cold arrange the bacon over the bottom of the flan and pour the egg mixture on top. Bake in a very

18

moderate oven for 30 minutes or until the pastry crust has browned and the egg mixture has set. Remove from the oven and store in a cool place overnight.

Next Day

Either serve cold, or reheat in a low oven. If you are eating the flan hot, you can cook it up to the end of stage 4 the day before, then do stage 5 just before you are ready to eat. This does mean you need to keep an eye on it, so it may be more convenient to complete the dish the day before.

The Day Before

Prawn Cheese and Bacon Flan

2 oz. cooked peeled prawns	(6)
2 rashers back bacon	(6)
1 oz. butter	(2½)
1 dessertspoon flour	(2½)
¼ pint milk	(⅔)
2 tablespoons grated mild English cheese	(6)
1 tablespoon sherry	(3)
½ egg-spoon French mustard	(1 teaspoon)
½ teaspoon chopped capers	(1½)
seasoning	
4½ oz. short crust pastry	(8)

Preparation

Cut the rind off the bacon. Grate the cheese. Chop the capers.

Action

1. Make the pastry (Appendix I), roll out and line a 5–6 in. (8–9 in.) flan case. Prick the bottom of the pastry all over with a fork, and in the middle lay a sheet of greased paper or foil on which you should put a handful of uncooked rice or dried beans to stop the pastry rising. Bake in a moderately hot oven

for 15 minutes, or until the pastry has set, but without brown-ing it.

2. While the flan case is cooking, fry the bacon in its own fat until crisp, then break it into small pieces.

3. Make a sauce with the butter, flour and milk. When the sauce has simmered for 4 minutes, withdraw the pan from the heat, stir in the prawns, cheese, bacon, sherry, mustard and capers. Mix thoroughly and season. Pour the mixture into a dish and allow it to cool. Cover and chill in the refrigerator overnight.

4. When the flan case is ready take it from the oven and remove the rice and foil. Cool and store in a cool place overnight.

Next Day

Fill the flan case with the prawn mixture and cook in a moderate oven for 20 (30) minutes, or until the pastry is lightly browned and the mixture really hot.

The Day Before

Crammed Ham

2 slices cooked ham	(6)
2 oz. liver pâté	(6)
2 oz. cream cheese	(6)
4 large prunes	(12)
seasoning	

Serve on a bed of chopped lettuce, tomatoes, and cucumber, brushed with a very small quantity of French dressing.

Preparation

Soak the prunes until they are juicy, then stone them. (You can leave them to soak until the next day and then stuff them at the last moment.) In any case a minimum of three hours is necessary.

Action

1. Mix together the liver pâté and cream cheese, and season.

2. Spread most of the mixture on to the ham, then make the ham into rolls or cornets. Stuff the prunes with the rest of the mixture, or, if you haven't had time to soak the prunes in advance, put the mixture into an airtight container in the refrigerator until the following day, and stuff them then.

3. Wrap the ham cornets and stuffed prunes in aluminium foil and store overnight in the refrigerator.

Next Day

Stuff the prunes if you did not do so the night before. Make a bed of lettuce, tomatoes and cucumber on a plate and arrange the ham rolls and prunes on top, and brush it all over with a very small quantity of French dressing. (Appendix I.)

The Day Before

Ham Truffle

2 oz. cooked ham	(6)
1 small onion	(2)
2 oz. mushrooms	(6)
1 large tomato	(3)
1 tablespoon double cream	(4)
1 dessertspoon flour	(2)
1½ oz. butter	(3)
¼ pint milk	(½)
½ small clove garlic	(1)
seasoning	
aspic or consommé with which to glaze (approximately 2 (6) tablespoons of either)	

Preparation

Peel and slice onion(s) and tomato(es), and finely chop garlic .

21

Wash and chop mushrooms. Remove any fat from the ham and discard it, then chop the meat.

Action

1. Melt ¾ (1½) oz. of the butter in a frying pan and sauté the onion(s), garlic, tomato(es) and mushrooms for 8 minutes, stirring occasionally.

2. If you have an electric blender, tip the contents of the pan into it, together with the chopped ham and cream. Otherwise, mince all the ingredients as finely as possible, then stir in the cream.

3. With the remains of the butter, the flour and milk, make a thick white sauce. Season with plenty of freshly ground black pepper. Add this sauce to the other ingredients in the blender and mix until smooth.

4. When the mixture is smooth, remove from the blender and adjust the seasoning. Pour the mixture into ramikin dishes and allow to cool, then spoon on the aspic (made up following the directions on the packet), or the consommé. (If the consommé is jellied when you take it out of the tin, warm slightly before using.) Chill in the refrigerator until required.

Note: Using consommé instead of aspic saves a lot of time and bother, but the only trouble is that in hot weather, if the food is taken out of the refrigerator more than a few minutes before serving, the consommé is liable to turn liquid again.

The Hour Before

Pineapple Pyre

2 slices pineapple (fresh if possible)	(6)
3 oz. cream cheese	(9)
2 oz. finely chopped smoked ham	(6)
1 tablespoon cream or top of milk	(3)
seasoning	

22

Preparation

Chop the smoked ham as finely as possible.

Action

1. Put the cream cheese in a bowl with the smoked ham and cream and mix thoroughly. Season well with freshly ground pepper.

2. Cut 2 (6) slices of pineapple. Remove the skin.

3. Put the pineapple slices on individual plates and put a portion of the cream cheese mixture on top of each. Garnish as required.

Note: This dish can be made perfectly well with tinned pineapple, but it does tend to be a little sweet, and fresh pineapple is very much nicer.

The Day Before

Bacon Queues

1 small tin sardines	(3)
4 rashers back bacon	(12)
1 oz. butter	(2½)
1 dessertspoon flour	(2½)
1 cup milk	(2½)
1½ tablespoons grated strong English Cheese	(5)
seasoning	

Preparation

Cut the rind off the bacon. Grate the cheese. Fillet the sardines if desired.

Action

1. Mash the sardines and spread them on the rashers of bacon. Roll the bacon up and put the rolls on skewers and cook them under the grill until the outside of the bacon is crisp.

2. Make a sauce with the butter, flour and milk. When the sauce has simmered for 4 minutes, withdraw the pan from the heat and stir in the cheese and season with freshly ground black pepper.

3. Arrange the bacon rolls in a shallow heatproof dish and withdraw the skewers. Pour the cheese sauce over them. Allow to cool and store in the refrigerator overnight.

Next Day

Reheat in a hot oven for 10 minutes.

The Day Before

Haddock Mousse

See 'Mains' section, p. 68.

The Day Before

Kipper Pâté

1 small kipper	(1 large)
2 oz. unsalted butter	(6)
1 tablespoon oil	(3)
1 tablespoon lemon juice	(3)
seasoning	

Serve with hot toast and butter or thinly sliced brown bread and butter.

Preparation

Leave butter out of the refrigerator to soften.

Action

1. Simmer the kipper for a few minutes in unsalted water. (To avoid the cooking smell, 'kippers in a bag' can be used and

cooked as directed on the packet, but the flavour isn't nearly so good.)

2. When the kipper is cooked, bone it very carefully—this is a long, boring and arduous task!

3. When all the bones have been extracted, mash the kippers as finely as possible with the butter, oil and lemon juice. Season with pepper, and add more lemon juice if necessary.

4. Pack the pâté into ramikin dishes and chill overnight in the refrigerator.

Next Day

Garnish with small sprigs of parsley.

The Day Before

Olive Roe

4 oz. cream cheese	(12)
2 oz. smoked cod's roe	(6)
2 large black olives	(6)
seasoning	
Serve with hot toast and butter	

Preparation

Remove the roe from the skin and take away any hard dry bits. Stone the olives.

Action

1. Mash the olives as finely as possible and blend with the cream cheese and cod's roe. Season if necessary.

2. Put the pâté into a dish and chill overnight in the refrigerator.

Note: This dish is fairly strong, so you want to be sure of your guests' tastes before producing it, but for those who are fond of olives, it is a very good starter.

The Day Before

Summer Pâté

2 oz. butter	(6)
4 oz. soft herring roes	(12)
¼ lemon (approx.)	(¾)
1 teaspoon chopped chives	(3)
seasoning	

Serve with hot toast and butter or with
brown bread and butter

Preparation

Wash and finely chop chives. Leave the butter to soften. Squeeze
the lemon.

Action

1. Melt 1 (3) oz. of the butter in a frying-pan and cook the roes
   for 5 minutes.

2. Tip the contents of the frying-pan into a bowl and beat the roes
   into a smooth paste, adding the rest of the butter, lemon juice,
   chives and seasoning.

3. Put the pâté into individual ramikin dishes and chill in the refrigerator until required.

Next Day

Garnish with a sprig of fresh parsley and perhaps a flurry of
paprika.

The Day Before

Tuna Fish Pâté

3½ oz. tin tuna fish	(12)
2 oz. butter	(6)
1 tablespoon olive oil	(3)
1 dessertspoon lemon juice	(3)
1 teaspoon grated onion	(2)
1 tablespoon brandy	(3)
seasoning	
Serve with hot toast and butter	

Preparation

Peel and grate the onion.

Action

1. If you have an electric blender, put the tuna fish, onion, butter, olive oil, lemon juice and brandy in and blend to a smooth cream. If not, mash the tuna fish and combine with the other ingredients until smooth.

2. Season and add more lemon juice if necessary. Put the pâté into a serving dish and garnish as required. Chill in the refrigerator until serving.

Suggested garnish: A sprinkling of grated hard-boiled egg.

The Day Before

Prawn and Cheese Pâté

3 oz. cream cheese	(10)
2 oz. cooked peeled prawns	(6)
2 teaspoons tomato ketchup	(6)
1 dessertspoon brandy	(3)
seasoning	
Serve with hot toast and butter	

Preparation

Nil.

Action

1. If you have an electric mixer or blender, blend together the cream cheese, shrimps and tomato ketchup. If not, mash the shrimps as finely as possible before mixing them with the cream cheese and tomato ketchup.

2. When the mixture is smooth, stir in the brandy and plenty of black pepper.

3. Put in a serving-dish and chill overnight. Garnish as required.

Suggested garnish: A few whole prawns arranged on top with small sprigs of parsley in between.

The Hour Before

Scrambled Prawns

3 eggs	(9)
2 oz. cooked peeled prawns	(6)
¾ oz. butter	(2½)
seasoning	
Serve on a bed of lettuce	

Preparation

Wash and lay out a good lettuce leaf on each plate. Break the eggs into a bowl and mix with a fork.

Action

1. Heat the butter in a saucepan and toss the prawns in it for 2 minutes.

2. Season the eggs and then pour them into the saucepan with the prawns. Scramble the eggs, stirring vigorously all the time

to keep the prawns well mixed in. Only cook the eggs until lightly scrambled, then divide into equal portions immediately and put on the lettuce leaves. Allow to cool, and garnish with a little paprika or parsley.

The Day Before

Muffled Prawns

2 oz. cooked peeled prawns	(6)
2 heaped tablespoons diced cucumber	(6)
½ oz. butter	(1½)
1 teaspoon flour	(1 tablespoon)
⅛ pint milk	(⅓)
1 tablespoon mayonnaise (see p. 208)	(3)
1 tablespoon grated mild English cheese	(3)
1 pinch paprika	(½ teaspoon)
seasoning	

Serve on a bed of shredded lettuce

Preparation

Skin the cucumber and dice the flesh into cubes of approximately ¼ in. Roughly chop the prawns if they are large. Grate the cheese. Wash the lettuce and put in refrigerator in airtight box or bag.

Action

1. Make a sauce with the butter, flour and milk. When the sauce has simmered for 4 minutes after coming to the boil, remove the pan from the heat and stir in the grated cheese and seasoning. Leave the sauce to get cold.

2. When the sauce has cooled, stir in the mayonnaise, then add the prawns and cucumber. Put the mixture in a covered bowl in the refrigerator overnight.

29

Next Day

Shred the lettuce and lay it as a bed in individual glasses. Spoon the mixture over it and sprinkle with paprika.

The Hour Before

Bonfire Melon

2 1-inch thick circular slices of honeydew melon	(6)
2 oz. cooked peeled shrimps or prawns	(6)
12 cashew nuts	(36)
3 tablespoons double cream	($\frac{1}{3}$ pint)
$\frac{1}{2}$ teaspoon curry powder	(1)

Preparation

Nil.

Action

1. Stir the curry powder into the cream, perhaps adding a little more according to your taste, then stir in the shrimps. (This part can be done the day before and left overnight in the refrigerator.)

2. Cut 2 (6) 1-in. thick circular slices of melon. Cut off the skin and remove the seeds.

3. Put the circles of melon on individual plates, with a portion of the prawn mixture in the centre, surrounded by the cashew nuts.

The Day Before

Prawn Delight

2 oz. cooked peeled prawns	(6)
1 egg	(3)
1 tomato	(3)
½ oz. butter	(1½)
½ dessertspoon flour	(1½)
½ cup milk	(1½)
1 dessertspoon Gruyère cheese	(3)
seasoning	

Preparation

Skin the tomato(es) and slice. Grate the cheese.

Action

1. Hard-boil the egg(s) and when cooked shell and slice.

2. While the egg(s) are boiling, make a sauce with the butter, flour and milk. When the sauce has simmered for 4 minutes, withdraw the pan from the heat and stir in the grated cheese and seasoning.

3. Butter 2 (6) ramikin dishes and arrange layers of prawns, tomato(es) and egg(s) and pour the cheese sauce over the top. Allow to cool, and chill in refrigerator overnight.

Next Day

Put small knobs of butter on top of each dish and heat in a hot oven for 10 minutes.

The Day Before

Marinated Prawns

4 oz. cooked peeled prawns	(12)
½ medium onion	(2)
4 bay leaves	(8)
4 dessertspoons oil	(8 tablespoons)
3 dessertspoons tarragon vinegar	(6 tablespoons)
¼ teaspoon salt	(¾)
1 pinch dry mustard	(½ teaspoon)
Serve on a bed of lettuce	

Preparation

Peel the onion(s) and slice very finely.

Action

1. In a small dish place a layer of prawns, then a layer of onions, topped with two bay leaves. Continue in similar layers until all the prawns are used up, finishing with an onion layer.

2. In a separate bowl combine the oil, vinegar, salt and mustard and pour this over the prawns.

3. Cover the dish and put it in the refrigerator for 24 hours.

Next Day

Drain the liquid from the prawns and serve individual portions on a bed of lettuce, removing the bay leaves as you do so.

The Hour Before

Rob's Prawns

4 oz. cooked peeled prawns	(12)
1½ oz. butter	(4)
1 small onion	(3)
1 teaspoon curry paste (see note)	(2½)
¼ pint single cream	(¾)
seasoning	
Serve with plain boiled rice	

Preparation

Peel and slice the onion(s), then chop finely. Wash rice.

Action

1. Heat the butter in a heavy saucepan and add the onion(s). Cover the pan and cook the onion(s) for 7 minutes, or until soft.

2. Add the prawns and curry paste. (If you only have curry powder, mix 1½ (4) teaspoons curry powder with 1 (3) tablespoons water.) Cook for 2 minutes, stirring constantly.

3. Transfer the contents of the saucepan to a casserole, and cook in a low oven for 15 minutes before you are ready to eat, and at the point of service stir in the cream. Return the dish to the oven for a few minutes to warm the cream, but do not allow it to boil.

4. At the same time as you put the casserole in the oven, put on a large pan of salt water to boil, and cook the rice when the water reaches boiling point, for 13 minutes. When cooked tip into a colander and run boiling water through it to separate the grains. It can then be left in a closed dish in a low oven without harm.

Note: Curry paste is bought ready made, and gives a more blended and slightly stronger flavour than curry powder. However, if this is not available, substitute the quantities of curry powder given in 2 above.

The Day Before

Prawn Coated Cauliflower

1 small cauliflower	(1 large)
4 oz. cooked peeled prawns	(12)
4 tablespoons (approx.) mayonnaise (see p. 208)	(12)
seasoning	

Preparation

Cut the leaves off the cauliflower, and a slice from the bottom so that it will stand flat on a plate, then soak in cold salt water to clean.

Action

1. Boil the cauliflower in salt water until just done. This is important as under no circumstances must the cauliflower be allowed to disintegrate. Drain and allow to get completely cold.

2. Cover the cauliflower with the prawns, sticking them in between the florets. Chill overnight in the refrigerator.

Next Day

At the point of service spoon the mayonnaise over the cauliflower and sprinkle with paprika.

The Day Before

Chelsea Tubs

5 inches (approx.) of cucumber	(15)
2 oz. cooked peeled shrimps	(6)
1 egg	(3)
½ teaspoon chopped chives	(1)
2 tablespoons mayonnaise (see p. 208)	(6)
seasoning	

Preparation

Skin the cucumber, then blanch it in boiling water for 2 minutes
and dry. Hard boil the egg(s). Chop the shrimps and chives.

Action

1. When you have blanched the cucumber, cut it into circles about
   1¼ in. thick. Scoop the seeds out from the centre, and put two
   circles of cucumber per person in a dish.

2. Chop the hard-boiled egg(s) and mix it in a bowl with the
   shrimps, chives, mayonnaise and seasoning.

3. Pile the egg and shrimp mixture into the centre of the
   cucumber and completely wrap the dish in foil before chilling
   overnight in the refrigerator.

Next Day

Transfer two circles of cucumber per person to small individual
plates and dust with paprika before serving.

The Day Before

Shrimp Surprise

2 oz. cooked peeled shrimps	(6)
1½ tablespoons grated Parmesan cheese	(5)
3 heaped tablespoons grated Gruyère cheese	(10)
2 dessertspoons consommé	(6)
⅛ pint double cream	(¼)
1 teaspoon lemon juice	(3)
seasoning	

Preparation

Grate the cheeses. Stiffly beat the cream.

Action

1. Put the grated cheeses into a bowl and add the cold consommé, lemon juice, and all but 2 (6) of the shrimps. Stir together.

2. Fold the stiffly beaten cream in with the other ingredients. Season and put the mixture into individual ramikin dishes. Garnish with the reserved shrimps, and as desired. Store in the refrigerator until you are ready to eat, otherwise the consommé may become liquid again in a warm room.

The Hour Before

Shrimp Pippin

1 small crisp apple	(2)
1 stick fresh celery	(3)
2 oz. cooked peeled shrimps	(6)
3 tablespoons double cream	($\frac{1}{4}$ pint)
1 teaspoon tomato ketchup	(4)
$\frac{1}{4}$ teaspoon Worcester sauce	(1)
seasoning	

Serve on a bed of shredded lettuce.

Preparation

Skin the apple(s) and celery and chop finely. Cut the shrimps in half. Shred the lettuce and put it in individual dishes to serve as a bed for the shrimps.

Action

1. Mix together the cream, tomato ketchup and Worcester sauce, adjusting to suit your own taste.

2. Add the shrimps, celery and apple(s) to the sauce. Season and pile the mixture on to the beds of lettuce. Garnish and chill until required.

Suggested garnish: thin slices of lemon cut into fan shapes.

The Day Before

Pâté Number One

¼ lb. chicken livers	(¾)
1 teaspoon grated onion	(3)
½ egg-spoon French mustard	(1 teaspoon)
2 tablespoons brandy	(4)
1½ oz. butter	(6)
1 bay leaf	(1)
1 pinch thyme	(1)
1 pinch marjoram	(1)
seasoning	

Serve with hot toast and butter.

Preparation

Peel and grate onion.

Action

1. Put the livers in a small saucepan with sufficient water to cover. Add the herbs. Cover the pan and cook over a very low heat for 15 minutes. Strain the livers, and reserve the stock for making soup.

2. Chop and mince the livers very finely, then blend them with the butter, grated onion, mustard and brandy. Season.

3. Put the mixture into a serving-dish and chill in the refrigerator overnight.

The Day Before

Pâté Number Two

2 oz. chicken livers	(6)
1 rasher streaky bacon	(3)
1 shallot	(3)
1½ oz. butter	(5)
1 teaspoon brandy	(3)
1 teaspoon port	(3)
seasoning	

Serve with hot toast and butter.

Preparation

Cut the rind off the bacon and cut the bacon into strips. Peel and finely chop the shallot(s).

Action

1. Put the bacon and the rinds in a frying-pan and cook over a low heat.

2. When the fat has run out of the bacon, add the shallot(s) and the chicken livers, and cook them lightly for about 5 minutes. (Use a little of the butter if the bacon has not produced enough fat.)

3. If you have a blender, put the contents of the frying-pan, with the exception of the bacon rind, into it. Add the butter, brandy, port and freshly ground black pepper, and blend until smooth.
   If you don't have a blender, you will have to discard the bacon, and mash the livers and shallot(s) as finely as possible before blending with the butter, brandy, port, and freshly ground black pepper.

4. Turn the pâté into a suitable dish and chill in the refrigerator until required.

The Day Before

Pork Pâté

¼ lb. pig's liver	(¾)
½ lb. belly of pork	(1¼)
1 chicken drumstick	(1 whole leg)
1 clove garlic	(2)
1 pinch mace	(1)
2 tablespoons white wine	(6)
1 dessertspoon brandy	(2)
1 pinch rosemary	(½ teaspoon)
seasoning	

Serve with hot toast and butter.

Preparation

Cut 4 (8) approx. slices of belly of pork from the piece, for use later to go over the top of the pâté, remove bones and cut off skin. Cut the skin off the rest of the belly of pork and bone, and do the same with the chicken. Peel the garlic and chop finely.

Action

1. Coarsely mince all the meat, except the strips of belly of pork being reserved.

2. Mix the meat with the garlic, mace, white wine, brandy, herb and seasoning. Leave for 1 hour for the flavour to develop.

3. After an hour put the mixture into a terrine or shallow pie dish, and lay the strips of belly of pork in a lattice on top.

4. Stand the dish in a pan of water, coming half to three-quarters way up the outside of the dish and cook in a very slow oven for 1¼ (1¾) hours, or until the pâté has shrunk about ¼ in. from the sides of the dish. The pâté should be covered with foil the first half hour of the cooking, and it is most important to cook it very slowly, otherwise it will dry up.

5. When cooked remove from the oven, cool, and chill in the refrigerator until required. It is best to keep the pâté for a day

or two, but it can be eaten straight away. If it is to be kept, run a little melted butter over the surface.

6. Before eating, turn the pâté out of its cooking-dish and serve on a bed of chopped lettuce.

The Day Before

Artichoke Soup

¾ lb. Jerusalem artichokes	(2 lbs.)
1 oz. ham	(3)
1 small onion	(2)
1 stick celery	(3)
1 oz. butter	(2½)
½ pint chicken stock	(1½)
½ pint milk	(1½)
1 bay leaf	(2)
1 blade mace	(1)
seasoning	

Serve with croûtons of fried bread.

Preparation
Peel and slice the artichokes, onion(s) and celery. Chop up the ham.

Action

1. In a large saucepan heat the butter and sauté the artichokes, ham and onion(s), and the celery, for 10 minutes, stirring occasionally, not letting them brown.

2. Add the stock, bay leaf, mace and seasoning. Cover the pan and simmer over a low heat for 30 minutes.

3. Extract the bay leaf and mace, and if you have an electric blender, pour the contents of the saucepan into it and mix until smooth. If not, sieve it.

4. Turn the soup into a bowl and chill overnight in the refrigerator.

Next Day

Make the fried bread croûtons and leave them in a heatproof dish
in the bottom of the oven until you are ready to eat.
Add the milk to the soup, adjust the seasoning and heat.

The Day Before

Cold Avocado Soup

1 small avocado pear	(2 large)
¼ small onion	(½)
⅓ small green pepper	(1)
½ oz. butter	(1½)
1½ teaspoons flour	(1 tablespoon)
¼ pint milk	(½)
½ pint chicken stock	(1½)
seasoning	

Preparation

Wash, deseed and shred green pepper. Peel and finely slice onion(s).

Action

1. Melt the butter in a thick saucepan over a low heat and add
   the pepper and onion. Cook for 10 minutes or just until the
   vegetables are soft, but take care not to let them brown.

2. Add the flour and cook for 2 minutes stirring constantly. Remove pan from heat and gradually stir in the milk. Return to
   heat and bring back to boil stirring constantly, then cook for
   2 minutes.

3. When the sauce has boiled for 2 minutes blend in the stock,
   and keep stirring until it returns to the boil. Cover and simmer
   for 15 minutes.

4. When the soup has simmered for almost 15 minutes, prepare
   the avocado pear(s) by slicing them in half, removing the

stone and scooping the flesh out into a bowl. Mash the flesh with a fork until it is quite smooth.

5. When the soup has simmered for 15 minutes, pour a little of it into the bowl with the avocado(s) and blend, then tip the contents into the saucepan. Season the soup and stir over the heat for a further two minutes, but do not allow it to boil.

6. Withdraw the pan from heat and if you have an electric blender, put the soup into it and mix until smooth. If not, push as much of it as you can through a fine sieve.

7. Allow to cool and then chill in the refrigerator until required.

The Day Before

Consommé Medley

2 cups tinned consommé	(6)
¼ avocado pear	(½)
1 medium-sized tomato	(3)
1 tablespoon diced cucumber	(3)
1 oz. peeled prawns	(3)
¼ teaspoon grated onion	(1)
2 tablespoons white wine vinegar	(5)
½ teaspoon olive oil	(1½)
¼ teaspoon Worcester sauce	(1)
seasoning	

Preparation

Peel, seed and chop tomato(es) and cucumber into small cubes. Peel and chop avocado pear and prawns. Peel and grate or very finely chop the onion.

Action

1. Combine all the ingredients in a large bowl and season. Pour the soup into individual soup cups and chill overnight in the

refrigerator. Leave in the refrigerator until you are ready to serve the soup, otherwise the consommé will turn liquid, whereas it should be lightly jellied.

The Day Before

Vichyssoise

1 large leek	(3)
1 medium potato	(3)
½ stick celery	(1)
¾ oz. butter	(1½)
½ pint chicken stock	(1½)
2 tablespoons double cream	(¼ pint)
seasoning	

Garnish with ½ teaspoon chopped chives per person.

Preparation

Cut the green part from the leek(s) and discard, then slice the white part in half and leave to soak for an hour or more. Peel the potato(es) and slice thinly. Scrape the celery and slice.

Action

1. Slice the leek(s) thinly and put them in a heavy saucepan with the butter. Cover the pan and cook for about 10 minutes, or until soft, and take care not to allow the leek(s) to brown.

2. Add the potato(es), celery and stock. Season, and simmer until all the vegetables are soft (about 20 minutes).

3. If you have a blender tip the contents of the pan into it and mix until smooth. If not, rub through a fine sieve.

4. Stir in the cream, adjust the seasoning and chill until required.

Next Day

Pour the soup into individual bowls and garnish with chopped chives or parsley.

Note: This soup can, of course, be eaten hot as well, and in this case it is better not to stir in the cream until you have reheated it.

The Day Before

Duncan's Soup

2 cups vichyssoise soup (see previous recipe)	(6)
½ cup chicken stock	(1½)
1 tablespoon sherry	(3)
½ medium-sized onion	(1)
½ small clove garlic	(1)
2 oz. peeled cooked shrimps	(6)
⅓ bunch watercress	(1)
¼ egg-spoon curry powder	(¾)
4 drops (approx.) Tabasco sauce	(10)
seasoning	
paprika	

If serving cold you also want 2 (6) dessertspoons commercially soured cream and 1 (3) teaspoons chopped chives.

Preparation

Make vichyssoise soup—see previous recipe; this may prove difficult in the summer on account of the general non-availability of leeks, and in this case substitute tinned vichyssoise in the recipe. Peel onion and garlic and chop roughly. Thoroughly wash the watercress and chop.

Action

1. Pour the vichyssoise into a large saucepan and add the chicken stock, onion, garlic, shrimps, watercress, Tabasco sauce, curry

powder and seasoning. Cover the pan and simmer gently for 30 minutes.

2. If you have an electric blender pour the soup into it and blend until smooth. If not, sieve it to make it really smooth, pushing through as much of the ingredients as possible.

3. Stir in the sherry and adjust seasoning.

4. Tip into some suitable container to store if you are going to have the soup hot, or if you are going to have it cold, which is better, pour it straight into the bowls and chill overnight in the refrigerator.

Next Day

If you are serving the soup hot, reheat it, and sprinkle on the paprika in the bowls when you are ready to serve.
If you are serving the soup cold, pour a spoonful of sour cream into each bowl; sprinkle on a few chopped chives, and dust with a flurry of paprika.

The Hour Before

Mussels in Mustard Soup

1 pint mussels	(3)
¾ pint court bouillon (Appendix I)	(2½)
1 glass white wine	(3)
½ teaspoon dry mustard	(1½)
2 egg yolks	(5)
seasoning	

Preparation

Make a court bouillon.
Scrub the mussels and discard any that are broken or open. Mix the mustard powder with a little of the court bouillon to make it smooth. Separate the egg yolks and whites.

45

Action

1. Strain the court bouillon into a very large saucepan and bring to the boil.

2. Add the mussels to it and cook until they are open. This takes about 2 minutes. Remove any that haven't opened as they may be bad.

3. Remove the pan from the stove and stir in the wine and mustard. Allow to cool slightly then pour a little of the mixture on to the egg yolks and mix, before adding to the pan. This avoids curdling or separating. Season the soup. Cover the pan and leave on the side until you go out to the kitchen to dish up.

4. At serving time reheat the soup, but do not boil. Put the mussels into large soup bowls and pour the soup over them.

Note: This is a very filling dish, and only something very light would be needed to follow.

The Day Before

Vegetable Soup

1 pint good meat stock	(3)
2 tomatoes	(6)
2 sticks celery	(6)
3 medium onions	(8)
½ carrot	(1)
4 sticks spaghetti	(12)
2 tablespoons oil	(6)
seasoning	

Serve with grated mild English cheese.

Preparation

Peel and slice the onions and tomatoes. Scrape and slice the celery and carrot. Grate the cheese and put it in an airtight container in the refrigerator until the next day.

Action

1. Heat the oil in a frying-pan and sauté the onions until they are soft and brown.

2. Transfer the onions to a saucepan, draining off any excess oil as you do so. Add the stock, the other vegetables, the spaghetti, which you should break into short pieces, and seasoning. Cover the pan and simmer for 2 hours.

3. Tip the soup into a suitable container and chill overnight in the refrigerator.

Next Day

Reheat and adjust the seasoning. Serve with the cheese.

The Day Before

Tomato Soup

4 large tomatoes	(12)
2 shallots	(5)
½ oz. butter	(1½)
1 dessertspoon flour	(3)
1 pint meat stock	(3)
1 glass white wine	(2)
1 pinch thyme	(½ teaspoon)
2 tablespoons single cream	(6)
seasoning	

Preparation

Peel and slice shallots. If you don't have an electric blender, skin the tomatoes; if you do, you needn't bother, just wash them. Then in either case chop them roughly.

Action

1. Heat the butter in a large saucepan and sauté the shallots for seven minutes.

2. Stir in the flour and cook for 2 minutes, stirring all the time. Withdraw the pan from the heat and blend in the stock and wine. Return to the flame and add the tomatoes, thyme and seasoning. Cover the pan and simmer for 1 hour.

3. If you have a blender, pour the soup in here and mix until smooth. If not, push it through a coarse sieve. Adjust the seasoning. Pour into a bowl and chill in refrigerator overnight.

Next Day

Pour the soup back into a saucepan and reheat. Pour a tablespoon of cream into each bowl as you serve it.

The Day Before

Artichoke Cheese

4 large fresh globe artichokes	(12)
or	
1 small tin of artichoke hearts	(3)
$\frac{3}{4}$ oz. butter	(2)
1 level dessertspoon flour	(2½)
$\frac{1}{4}$ pint milk	($\frac{3}{4}$)
$\frac{1}{3}$ wine-glass white wine	(1)
2 tablespoons grated mild English cheese	(6)
seasoning	

If you are using fresh artichokes, you will also need 1 dessert-spoon oil and 1 tablespoon lemon juice.

Preparation

If using fresh artichokes, which are that much better, but vastly more trouble, soak them in salt water for an hour or two before cooking. When they have soaked, boil them in salted water with the lemon juice and oil added, until the leaves will pull off (about 40–50 minutes). Remove all the leaves and cut out the artichoke hearts, taking care to take off all the hairs forming the choke bit on top. Grate the cheese.

Action

1. Make a sauce with the butter, flour and milk. When the sauce has simmered for 4 minutes, stir in the wine and simmer for 5 minutes. Then withdraw the pan from the heat and stir in the cheese and seasoning.

2. Put the artichoke hearts in a heatproof dish. Pour over the sauce and allow to cool before chilling in the refrigerator overnight.

Next Day

Bake in a hot oven for 10–15 minutes.

The Day Before

Stuffed Aubergine

1 long-shaped fresh aubergine	(3)
½ small onion	(1 medium)
2 large tomatoes	(1½)
1 small clove garlic	(6)
2 tablespoons oil	(6)
1 bay leaf	(2)
1 pinch basil	(½ teaspoon)
seasoning	

Preparation

Cut the aubergine(s) in half, lengthways, and put them to soak in salt water for at least half an hour. Put a plate or something on top of them to prevent them floating. Peel and grate the onion. Peel and very finely slice the garlic. Skin and chop the tomatoes.

Action

1. Put the aubergine(s) in a saucepan with the bay leaf, seasoning and sufficient water to cover, bring to the boil and simmer gently for 12 minutes.

49

2. When the aubergine(s) are cooked drain them and remove most of the pulp, but leaving a layer about ⅛ in. thick all round.

3. Put the pulp into a bowl of water and chop it. In this way the pips and pulp will separate, and you can extract the pulp only.

4. Drain the pulp and put it in a bowl with the tomato, onion and garlic and mash it all together. Sprinkle on the basil and seasoning and add the oil. Mix again.

5. Stuff the aubergine(s) with the mixture. Put them in a lidded dish and chill in the refrigerator until required.

The Hour Before

Spicy Avocado

2 avocado pears	(5)
1 small tomato	(3)
½ chilli pepper	(1½)
1 tablespoon olive oil	(3)
1 teaspoon vinegar	(3)
1 teaspoon lemon juice	(3)
½ small green pepper	(1 medium)
seasoning	

Preparation

Skin, deseed and mash the tomato(es), green pepper and chilli pepper(s) as finely as possible. Mix together the oil, vinegar, lemon juice and seasoning.

Action

1. Cut the avocado pears in half; remove the stones and scoop the flesh out into a bowl, taking care to preserve 2 (6) half shells.

2. Mash the avocado pears together with the tomato(es), green pepper and chilli pepper(s). Moisten them with the dressing

and pile the mixture back into the reserved shells. Cover with foil until required.

Note: This is also an excellent cocktail dip when served with potato crisps or lightly flavoured small biscuits.

The Day Before

Stuffed Courgettes

2 large courgettes	(6)
2–3 tablespoons cold minced meat or poultry	(6–8)
1 shallot	(3)
1 tomato	(3)
seasoning	

Preparation

Mince any kind of left-over meat or poultry. (The quantity needed depends on the size of the courgettes you are using.) Skin the tomato(es) and shallot(s) and chop very finely. Wash the courgettes. Cut off the ends and reserve. Scoop out the centres with a potato peeler or apple corer.

Action

1. Mix together the minced meat, shallot(s), tomato(es) and seasoning.
2. Stuff the courgettes with the mixture, and put the reserved ends back on to keep the stuffing in place.
3. Butter a sheet of foil and wrap the courgettes in it. Store in the refrigerator overnight.

Next Day

Put the parcel of courgettes into a heat-proof open dish and bake in a moderate oven for 1 hour.

Note: You could cook the courgettes the day before and eat them cold.

The Hour Before

Crossed Courgettes

4 medium-sized courgettes	(12)
1 small onion	(2)
3 tomatoes	(8)
1½ oz. butter	(3)
2 oz. grated Cheddar cheese	(4)
seasoning	

Preparation

Wash and slice the courgettes into half-inch pieces. Peel and slice the tomatoes. Peel and finely chop the onion(s). Grate the cheese. Butter a pie-dish.

Action

1. In a frying-pan heat the butter and sauté the courgettes for 10 minutes. Remove them all from the pan and put half in the buttered pie-dish. Keep the other half on one side.

2. Add the onion(s) and tomatoes to the remainder of the butter in the pan and sauté them for 7 minutes.

3. Sprinkle half the cheese on the courgettes in the dish and a little seasoning. Then add a layer of tomato and onion, followed by a layer of the remaining courgettes. Season again and top off with the rest of the grated cheese.

4. Bake in a moderate oven for 35 minutes.

The Hour Before

Mushroom Cocktail

¼ lb. fresh button mushrooms	(¾)
¼ small onion	(½)
1 tablespoon mayonnaise (see p. 208)	(3)
⅛ pint double cream	(⅓)
1½ teaspoons anchovy essence	(1 tablespoon)
seasoning	

Serve with brown bread and butter and a wedge of
lemon.

Preparation

Wash and slice the mushrooms. Peel and very finely chop the
onion. Lightly whip the cream.

Action

1. Combine the mayonnaise, cream, onion and anchovy essence.
   Season, and chill the sauce for 30 minutes.

2. Stir the mushrooms into the sauce and put into individual
   glasses, and place in the refrigerator until you are ready to
   serve.

The Hour Before

Filled Mushrooms

6 large flat mushrooms	(18)
1 rasher streaky bacon	(3)
½ cup fresh white breadcrumbs	(1½)
2 tablespoons oil	(6)
⅓ cup grated mild English cheese	(1)
seasoning	

53

Preparation

Wash the mushrooms and finely chop the stalks. Make the fresh breadcrumbs. Grate the cheese. Very finely chop the bacon, having removed rind.

Action

1. Knead together the bacon, mushroom stalks, breadcrumbs, cheese and seasoning.

2. Lay the mushrooms, brown side up, in an ovenproof dish. Pile equal quantities of the mixture into each mushroom, and pour a little of the olive oil over each.

3. Cover the dish and bake in a moderate oven for 30 minutes.

The Day Before

Mushroom Salad

2 oz. button mushrooms	(6)
2 dessertspoons diced cucumber	(6)
1 egg	(3)
2 tomatoes	(6)
⅛ pint commercially soured cream	(½)
⅓ teaspoon dry mustard	(1)
seasoning	

Preparation

Hard boil the egg(s). Skin the tomatoes and cucumber. Wash the mushrooms very carefully.

Action

1. Finely chop the hard-boiled egg(s), mushrooms, cucumber and tomatoes.

2. Mix all the above ingredients together and season.

3. Blend the mustard with the sour cream and stir it into the other ingredients. Chill overnight in the refrigerator.

Next Day

Transfer equal portions of the salad to individual glasses and serve as you would a prawn cocktail.

The Day Before

Stuffed Peppers

2 medium-sized round green peppers	(6)
1 small onion	(3)
4 oz. fresh lean minced beef	(12)
2 tablespoons fresh white breadcrumbs	(6)
2 tomatoes	(6)
1 pinch basil	($\frac{1}{2}$ teaspoon)
1 dessertspoon oil	(2)
seasoning	

Preparation

Cut the end off the peppers, removing any seeds and reserve. Deseed the whole peppers. Peel and slice the onion(s) and tomatoes finely. Make the breadcrumbs.

Action

1. Heat the oil in a frying-pan and sauté the onion(s) until soft.

2. Add the minced beef, tomatoes and breadcrumbs to the onion(s) in the frying-pan and cook, stirring frequently, for 7 minutes. Sprinkle on the basil and seasoning and mix thoroughly. Withdraw the pan from the heat and allow the mixture to cool.

3. Stuff the peppers with the mixture in the frying-pan. Place the stuffed peppers on a sheet of foil in an open ovenproof dish.

Replace the reserved ends on the peppers, and put the dish to cool completely before chilling overnight in the refrigerator.

Next Day

Bake the peppers in a low oven for 1 hour, and when cooked slide them from the foil on to individual plates to serve.

The Day Before

Ratatouille

1 small onion	(2)
1 clove garlic	(2)
1 aubergine	(3)
1 green pepper	(3)
1 large courgette	(3)
4 large ripe juicy tomatoes	(12)
½ egg-spoon basil	(1½)
3 tablespoons olive oil	(8)
seasoning	

Preparation

Peel and coarsely dice onion(s), tomatoes and aubergine(s), then cover the latter with salt and leave in a colander with a weighted plate on top for 30 minutes to remove excess bitterness. Wash, deseed and coarsely dice the green pepper(s). Wash and coarsely dice courgette(s). Peel and chop garlic.

Action

1. Heat the oil in a heavy saucepan and simmer the onion(s) and garlic for 7 minutes.

2. Rinse and pat dry the aubergine(s) after 30 minutes, and add these and the green pepper(s) to the pan. Cover and cook for 10 minutes, stirring occasionally.

3. Add the courgette(s), cover the pan again and continue cooking for 15 minutes.

4. Add the tomatoes, basil and seasoning, cover and cook for another 30 minutes. Stir occasionally to make sure the vegetables aren't sticking.

5. After cooking transfer to a serving-dish if you are going to eat the ratatouille cold, or to a casserole if you are going to eat it hot. Cool, and chill overnight in the refrigerator.

Next Day

Either serve cold, or reheat in a low oven.

Note: If you can't buy really juicy tomatoes, it is better to substitute ¾ (2) cup(s) tinned tomatoes.

The Hour Before

Stuffed Tomatoes

4 large tomatoes	(12)
4 flat mushrooms	(12)
1 tablespoon fresh white breadcrumbs	(4)
1 shallot	(3)
1 small stick celery	(2 ordinary)
1 teaspoon mixed herbs	(3)
1 oz. butter	(2½)
¾ oz. garlic butter	(2)
2 slices of bread	(6)
1 tablespoon milk	(4)
seasoning	

Preparation

Make the garlic butter by adding a little squeezed garlic, or garlic powder, to the butter and mixing thoroughly. Cut the crusts off the bread and make the slices circular. Peel the mushrooms, and

chop up the peel and the stalks. Skin the shallot(s) and celery
and chop very finely. Make the breadcrumbs. If using fresh
herbs (parsley, thyme and basil, are best) chop them finely. Cut
the tops off the tomatoes and scoop out the seeds.

Action

1. Put the breadcrumbs into a dish with the milk and allow them
   to soak for 5 minutes. Add a little more milk if necessary.

2. Heat half the butter in a frying-pan and sauté the mushroom
   stalks and peel, the celery, and the shallot(s) for 5 minutes.

3. Add the herbs, breadcrumbs and seasoning to the ingredients
   in the pan and cook for a further 5 minutes, stirring constantly.

4. Stuff the tomatoes with the mixture in the frying-pan and put
   a whole mushroom on top of each.

5. Toast the bread and spread it with garlic butter. Lay the pieces
   of toast in a fireproof dish and put the tomatoes on top.

6. Put dabs of the remaining butter on top of the mushrooms,
   then cover them with buttered paper.

7. Cook in a hot oven for 10 minutes.

The Hour Before

Tomato Crunch

4 medium tomatoes	(12)
4 oz. cream cheese	(12)
¾ oz. chopped walnuts	(2)
seasoning	

Preparation

Cut the tops off the tomatoes and scoop out the seeds with a
teaspoon. Turn the shells upside down to drain until required.
Finely chop the walnuts.

Action

1. Mix together the cream cheese and walnuts and season well with freshly ground black pepper.

2. Stuff the cream cheese mixture into the tomatoes and chill until required.

Suggestions for Additional First Courses Requiring no Recipes

There are a number of additional first courses suitable for inclusion in this book, but we have not mentioned them in the preceding pages because they require no recipes to make them. However, in order to help you plan your meals, we thought it would be useful to list them here.

Soups

Consommé (tinned), either hot or jellied with a little sherry added.
Turtle Soup (tinned), with sherry added and cheese straws as accompaniment.
Lobster Bisque (tinned), with brandy and cream added.

Hors d'œuvre

Include dishes of eggs, sardines, baked beans, anchovies, sweetcorn, artichoke hearts, tomatoes, potato salad, salami, olives, and anything else liked.

Eggs

Egg Mayonnaise.
Gulls' Eggs (in season) ⎱ serve both with brown bread and
Plovers' Eggs (in season) ⎰   butter and celery salt.

Fish

Dublin Bay Prawns with mayonnaise.
Fresh Shrimps—serve with brown bread and butter.
Potted Shrimps—serve with hot toast and butter.

Oysters—serve with brown bread and butter, lemon, red pepper and Tabasco sauce.

Smoked Salmon
Smoked Trout
Smoked Eel   serve all with brown bread and butter and
Smoked Buckling   lemon.
Smoked Herrings
Smoked Sprats

Fruit

Grapefruit.
Charantais Melon.
Ogen Israel Melon.
Honeydew Melon and Parma Ham.

Vegetables

Avocado Pear with French dressing.
Avacado Pear stuffed with salmon, crab or prawns.
Avacado Pear with watercress chopped up in a French dressing.
Avacado Pear stuffed with cream cheese to which has been added finely-chopped ham.
Globe Artichokes served hot with butter.
Globe Artichokes served cold with mayonnaise.
Asparagus served cold with mayonnaise.

Liver Pâtés

Many varieties of liver pâté can be bought in delicatessen shops or supermarkets, and can be served with hot buttered toast or French bread.

Mains

The Day Before

Egg and Bacon Pie

3 eggs	(9)
4 rashers back bacon	(12)
½ oz. butter	(1½)
1 level dessertspoon flour	(2)
¼ pint milk	(⅔)
2 tablespoons grated mild English cheese	(6)
seasoning	
4½ oz. short-crust pastry	(8)

Preparation

Cut the rinds off the bacon. Grate the cheese.

Action

1. Make the pastry and leave in the refrigerator (Appendix I).

2. Hard-boil the eggs, shell and slice, and put in a buttered pie-dish.

3. Fry the bacon until crisp in its own fat and cut into pieces and put with the eggs in the pie-dish.

4. Make a thick white sauce with the butter, flour and milk. When the sauce has simmered for 4 minutes, withdraw from the heat, season and stir in the cheese. Pour the sauce over the bacon and eggs and allow to cool completely.

5. When the mixture is cool, roll out the pastry (which should be removed from refrigerator half an hour before it is needed) to cover the pie-dish, and when covered store the pie in the refrigerator overnight.

Next Day

Bake in a hot oven for 20–25 (25–30) minutes.

The Day Before

Egg and Tomato Crumble

4 eggs	(12)
3 medium tomatoes	(9)
1 large onion	(3)
1½ oz. butter	(2)
2 tablespoons grated strong English cheese	(6)
2 tablespoons fresh white breadcrumbs	(6)
1 teaspoon castor sugar	(1 tablespoon)
seasoning	

Preparation

Peel and slice onion(s) and tomatoes. Make breadcrumbs. Grate cheese.

Action

1. Boil the eggs until hard. Peel and slice.

2. Sauté the onion(s) in ¾ (1¼) oz. of the butter for 10 minutes, or until soft, taking care not to allow them to brown.

3. Butter a heatproof dish and put in it layers of onion, egg and tomato, seasoning each layer with salt and pepper and the tomato layers with the sugar as well. Continue until all the ingredients are used up.

4. Mix together the grated cheese and breadcrumbs and sprinkle over the dish. Dot with the rest of the butter.

Next Day

Bake in a moderately hot oven for 30 minutes, browning the top under the grill if necessary.

The Day Before

Egg Cutlets

5 eggs	(14)
2 rashers streaky bacon	(6)
½ teaspoon chopped chives	(2)
½ oz. butter	(2)
1 dessertspoon flour	(3)
¼ pint milk	(½)
seasoning	
breadcrumbs	
fat for deep frying	

Preparation

Hard boil 4 (12) of the eggs, saving the others for coating the completed cutlets. Chop the chives. Dice the bacon finely.

Action

1. Fry the bacon until it is crisp, then put it in a bowl with the chives. Chop the hard-boiled eggs and add these.

2. Make a thick white sauce with the butter, flour, milk and seasoning. Pour the sauce into the bowl with the other ingredients. Mix thoroughly and allow to cool.

3. When the mixture has cooled, turn it out on to a plate and divide into equal portions, allowing two portions per person.

4. Beat up the remaining egg(s) in a plate, and prepare a paper, or plate if you prefer, with the breadcrumbs. Also have a floured board or plate on which to shape the cutlets.

5. Make each portion into shapes resembling lamb cutlets on your floured board. Then dip in the egg and breadcrumbs.

6. Deep-fry the cutlets. Allow to cool, and store in refrigerator overnight.

Next Day

Put the cutlets in an open ovenproof dish and reheat in a low oven.

Note: Half quantities would make enough for a starter.

General Notes on Choosing Fish

When buying fresh or salt water fish you can tell if they are really fresh if they have bright clear eyes; the gills should be bright red and the flesh firm. Fish should never have an unpleasant odour.

All the recipes using shell fish, in this book, are for fish that has already been cooked and your fishmonger should do this for you.

Generally speaking, Monday is not a good day to buy fresh fish as the boats have not been out over the week end, and in many parts of the country, for this reason, fishmongers are closed that day.

The Day Before

Crunchy Fish Pie

¾ lb. fresh haddock	(2)
2 tomatoes	(6)
2 oz. mushrooms	(6)
½ small green pepper	(1)
½ oz. butter[1]	(1½)
1 dessertspoon flour	(2½)
⅛ pint milk	(⅓)
⅛ pint water	(⅓)
3 tablespoons fresh white breadcrumbs	(9)
1 dessertspoon Parmesan cheese	(3)
seasoning	

Preparation

Skin the tomatoes and chop. Wash the mushrooms and slice. Wash green pepper, deseed and chop very finely. Make the breadcrumbs.

---

[1] You will also need butter or lard in which to fry the breadcrumbs, but it would be difficult to give the exact amount.

Action

1. Put the fish into a saucepan with the milk, water and some black pepper. Bring to the boil and simmer for 7 minutes.

2. While the fish is cooking, heat some butter or lard in a frying-pan and fry the breadcrumbs gently until they are crisp, taking care not to let them burn, then put them in a bowl and mix with the Parmesan cheese.

3. When the fish is cooked, strain the liquid into a jug. Extract the bones and the skin from the fish and put the flaked fish into a pie-dish.

4. Heat the butter in a saucepan and lightly sauté the mushrooms, then put them with the fish.

5. Stir the flour into the butter in which the mushrooms were cooked and make a sauce with the fish stock. When the sauce has simmered for 4 minutes, withdraw from the heat and season. Pour the sauce over the fish and add the tomatoes and green pepper and stir well.

6. Allow the pie to cool, then sprinkle on the mixture of breadcrumbs and cheese, and chill overnight in the refrigerator.

Next Day
Reheat the pie thoroughly in a hot oven.

The Day Before

Haddock Monte Carlo

¾ lb. smoked haddock	(2)
4 medium tomatoes	(12)
2 oz. mushrooms	(6)
2 oz. grated mild English cheese	(4)
1½ oz. butter	(3½)
1 heaped dessertspoon flour	(2½)
½ pint milk	(1)
1 teaspoon lemon juice	(3)
seasoning	

Preparation

Trim the haddock and soak for 30 minutes in water to remove the
excess salt. Peel and slice the tomatoes. Wash and slice the mushrooms. Grate the cheese.

Action

1. After the haddock has soaked, put it in a saucepan with the
   milk and some black pepper and simmer for 10 minutes.

2. Whilst the fish is cooking, sauté the mushrooms in $\frac{1}{2}$ ($1\frac{1}{2}$) oz.
   of the butter, and sprinkle with the lemon juice. Leave on one
   side.

3. When the fish is cooked, strain the milk into a jug and leave
   the fish to cool while you make a sauce with the butter, flour
   and the milk. When the sauce has simmered for 4 minutes,
   withdraw the pan from the heat and stir in the cheese and
   season.

4. Bone and flake the haddock. Put the flaked fish into an ovenproof dish with the sliced tomatoes and mushrooms. Pour the
   sauce over and mix well. Allow to cool, and chill overnight
   in the refrigerator.

Next Day

Reheat thoroughly in a low oven.

The Day Before

Haddock Mousse

10 oz. smoked haddock	(2 lb.)
1 egg yolk	(3)
2 egg whites	(5)
1 oz. butter	($2\frac{1}{2}$)
1 level dessertspoon flour	($2\frac{1}{2}$)
1 cup milk	(2)
$\frac{1}{4}$ pint double cream	($\frac{1}{2}$)
seasoning	

Preparation

Wash and trim the haddock and soak for half an hour to remove excess salt. Separate the egg yolks and whites. Whip the cream.

Action

1. Place the haddock in a saucepan with the milk and some freshly ground black pepper. Bring it to the boil and simmer for 7 minutes. Strain the juice into a jug, and put the fish on a plate to cool.

2. While the fish is cooling sufficiently to handle, make a very thick white sauce with the butter, flour and ½ (1) cup of the liquid in which the fish was cooked. When the sauce has simmered for 4 minutes, withdraw the pan from the heat and leave it to cool while you bone the fish, which should then be mashed as finely as possible.

3. Stir the egg yolk(s) into the sauce (one at a time), then add the fish and stir until smooth. When it is smooth mix in the whipped cream.

4. Whisk the egg whites until stiff and fold these in. Adjust the seasoning, pour the mixture into a soufflé dish and chill in the refrigerator until needed.

Next Day

Garnish with perhaps slices of tinned red peppers cut into patterns, such as bunches of cherries, flowers, etc. and use cucumber skin for stalks and leaves.

Note: This dish makes a good first course in a smaller quantity and should be served with brown bread and butter. The quantity given above for 2 is sufficient as a first course for 4 if served in individual ramikins.

The Hour Before

Stuffed Herrings

2 herrings	(6)
2 oz. mushrooms	(4)
1 dessertspoon chopped onion	(2)
1 dessertspoon fresh white breadcrumbs	(4)
½ teaspoon lemon juice	(2)
1 oz. butter	(2½)
seasoning	

Preparation

Gut and bone the herrings. (You can get the fishmonger to do this for you, but it is quite an easy operation.) Chop up the roes. Make the breadcrumbs. Peel and finely chop the onion(s). Wash and finely chop the mushrooms.

Action

1. Mix together the chopped roes, mushrooms and onion(s).

2. Heat the butter in a frying-pan and lightly fry the roe mixture for about 5 minutes.

3. Withdraw the pan from the heat and mix in the breadcrumbs, lemon juice and seasoning.

4. Spread the mixture on to the boned herrings. Fold them over and lay them completely wrapped in tin foil, in an open oven-proof dish.

5. Cook for 40 minutes in a medium oven, then turn right down until you are ready to eat.

Note: This dish can only be made at the time of year when roes are in season, but either hard or soft herring roes can be used.

The Hour Before

Horseradish Fish

¾ lb. white fish	(2 lb.)
2 tablespoons prepared horseradish sauce	(5)
¼ cup softened butter	(¾)
⅛ pint single cream	(½)
seasoning	

Preparation

Trim the fish, removing the skin and any visible bones, and cut it into pieces. Soften the butter.

Action

1. Butter a casserole and put in it a layer of fish smeared with butter and horseradish sauce, and continue in the same way until all the fish is used up.

2. Season the fish and pour the cream over the top.

3. Cover the dish and cook for 35 minutes in a moderate oven.

The Day Before

Kedgeree

6 oz. smoked haddock	(1¼ lb.)
1 hard-boiled egg	(3)
2 rashers of streaky bacon	(6)
2 oz. mushrooms	(6)
3 tablespoons uncooked long-grain rice	(9)
4 oz. butter	(8)
1 tablespoon fresh chopped parsley	(3)
seasoning	

Preparation

Trim the haddock and soak it for 30 minutes in cold water to

71

get rid of the excess salt. Wash the rice and mushrooms and slice the latter. Cut the rind from the bacon.

Action

1. Simmer the haddock in enough water to cover for 10 minutes.

2. At the same time boil the rice for 13 minutes in a large pan of boiling salt water. Test to make sure it is cooked after 13 minutes, but it should be perfect. When cooked tip the rice into a sieve and run boiling water through it to separate the grains, then drain it and put it in a bowl. Cover it with foil and store in the refrigerator.

3. Also at the same time hard boil the egg(s) and when cooked, peel and chop.

4. Fry the bacon until crisp and break it into small pieces. Sauté the mushrooms in the resulting fat. When cooked put in a bowl with the bacon and egg(s).

5. When the fish has cooked, allow it to cool slightly for easier handling, then extract the bones and flake the fish into the bowl with all the other ingredients except the rice. Mix together and season. Cover the bowl with foil and store in the refrigerator overnight.

Next Day

Mix the rice and other ingredients together and put them in a casserole with the butter, and heat thoroughly in a low oven. While the dish is warming, chop the parsley and at the point of service sprinkle it over the dish.

The Day Before

Salmon Mousse

½ lb. fresh salmon	(1½)
1 egg	(3)
¾ oz. butter	(2)
⅓ packet aspic	(1)
2 level dessertspoons flour	(4)
⅛ pint milk	(¼)
1 glass white wine	(2)
2 tablespoons single cream	(6)
1 dessertspoon lemon juice	(3)
1 slice lemon	(1)
1 bay leaf	(2)
1 sprig thyme	(1)
seasoning	

Preparation

Separate the egg yolk(s) and white(s). Cut a slice from a lemon and squeeze some juice from the rest of it.

Action

1. Put the salmon in a large saucepan or fish kettle with the wine, slice of lemon, bay leaf, thyme, seasoning and sufficient water to cover. Bring the liquid to the boil and simmer for 15–20 (30–40) minutes, or until the fish is cooked.

2. When the fish is cooked, strain the liquid into a jug. Make up the aspic using ¼ (½) pint of the fish stock to do so. Leave it to cool.

3. Make a thick white sauce with the butter, flour, milk and ¼ (⅔) pint of the fish stock. After the sauce has simmered for 4 minutes, withdraw the pan from the heat and tip a little of the sauce on to the egg yolk(s) and mix, before adding them to the pan. Add the lemon juice and seasoning.

4. Bone and skin the salmon. Then, if you have an electric blender, put the fish and sauce into it and blend until smooth. Otherwise,

mash up the fish as finely as possible before adding it to the
sauce.

5. When the mixture is smooth, stir in the cream and aspic.
   Whip the egg white(s) until they are stiff, then fold them in.
   Adjust seasoning. Pour the mixture into a wet soufflé dish or
   mould, and chill in the refrigerator overnight.

Next Day

Tip the mousse out of the dish. This should be quite easy if the
dish was wet when you put the mixture in; however, if you have
trouble, loosen round the edges with a palette knife and stand
the dish in a bowl of warm water for about 30 seconds.

Garnish with very thin slices of peeled cucumber (this is most
easily done with a potato-peeler), laid overlapping in a circle round
the rim of the mousse, and a smaller circle of overlapping cucumber slices in the middle with a small sprig of parsley in the middle
of this. It also looks attractive served on a bed of chopped lettuce.

The Day Before

Cold Salmon

¾ lb. fresh salmon	(2 lb.)
1 wine glass white wine	(2)
¼ lemon	(½)
1 sprig thyme	(1)
1 bay leaf	(2)
2 black peppercorns	(4)

Serve with home-made mayonnaise (see p.
208), a sliced cucumber salad, and Webbs
Wonderful, Iceburg or similar crisp lettuce.

Preparation

Wrap the salmon in a piece of muslin to facilitate its removal
from the saucepan when cooked.

Action

1. Place the salmon in a saucepan. Cover it with water and add
   the wine, lemon, thyme, bay leaf and peppercorns. Put the lid
   on the pan; bring the water up to boiling point and keep it
   there for 1 (5) minutes, then turn off the heat and leave the
   salmon in the liquid until it is completely cold.

2. While the salmon is cooking, wash the lettuce and put it in a
   polythene bag in the refrigerator to crisp. Slice the cucumber,
   reserving a little for the decoration of the salmon next day,
   and cover it with vinegar. Put it in a dish in the refrigerator
   until required. Make the mayonnaise.

3. When the salmon is cold, lift it out of the pan with the muslin
   and put it somewhere very cool overnight.

Next Day

Unwrap the salmon and remove the skin. Put it on a serving-dish
and decorate with a little of the mayonnaise and a few slices of
cucumber.

The Day Before

Cold Salmon Kedgeree

6 oz. salmon	(1¼ lb.)
2 tablespoons rice	(6)
1 teaspoon grated onion	(3)
6 capers	(18)
1 egg	(3)
1 carrot	(1)
1 bay leaf	(1)
2 tablespoons mayonnaise (see p. 208)	(6)
2 tablespoons single cream	(6)
1 tablespoon lemon juice	(3)
seasoning	

75

Preparation

Skin and grate the onion(s). Skin the carrot and chop in half. Chop the capers. Make mayonnaise if necessary. Wash the rice. Trim the salmon.

Action

1. Cook salmon as in previous recipe omitting wine, lemon, thyme and peppercorn but putting in the carrot. Boil for 1 minute with the smaller piece and 3 minutes with the larger.

2. While the salmon is cooking, boil the rice in plenty of salt water, and hard boil the egg(s) and chop.

3. When the salmon is cold, remove all the bones and flake the meat into a large bowl. Add the rice, egg, capers and onion. Cover the bowl with foil and chill in refrigerator overnight.

Next Day

Mix the ingredients together thoroughly and bind together with the mayonnaise and cream. Add the lemon juice and season to taste. Transfer to a serving-dish and garnish with perhaps slices of lemon cut into quarters and laid in fan shapes in the centre with small sprigs of parsley round them.

The Hour Before
Crab Casserole

½ lb. fresh or frozen crab meat	(1½)
1 large pickled gherkin	(3)
1 tablespoon chopped red pepper	(3)
1 tablespoon chopped green olives	(3)
2 oz. mushrooms	(6)
1 cup fresh white breadcrumbs	(3)
2 oz. butter	(4)
1 dessertspoon flour	(2 tablespoons)
½ pint milk	(1½)
1 teaspoon tomato ketchup	(3)
2 tablespoons grated mild English cheese	(6)
seasoning	

76

Preparation

Chop the gherkin(s) and olives. Extract all the bones from the crab. Wash and slice the mushrooms. Make the breadcrumbs. Grate the cheese. Wash, deseed and chop red pepper.

Action

1. Make a sauce with the butter, flour and milk. Simmer for 4 minutes then withdraw from the heat and stir in all the other ingredients, except the cheese. Season.

2. Butter a casserole and transfer the contents of the saucepan to it. Sprinkle on the grated cheese and bake in a moderate oven for 30 (40) minutes.

The Hour Before

Scallops in Wine and Cheese

4 large scallops	(12)
2 oz. mushrooms	(6)
1 large tomato	(3)
2 oz. butter	(4)
1 tablespoon flour	(2)
2 tablespoons sherry	(6)
$\frac{1}{4}$ pint milk	($\frac{3}{4}$)
2 tablespoons grated mild English cheese	(6)
seasoning	

Preparation

Wash and slice mushrooms. Skin and slice tomato(es). Grate the cheese.

Action

1. Put the scallops into boiling salted water for 1 minute, then drain them and put them in a baking-dish.

2. Heat a little of the butter in a frying-pan and sauté the mushrooms. Put on one side.

3. Make a sauce with the rest of the butter, the flour and the milk. When the sauce has simmered for 4 minutes, withdraw the pan from the heat and stir in the sherry, mushrooms, tomato(es) and seasoning.

4. Pour the sauce over the scallops. Sprinkle on the grated cheese, and put the dish in a hot oven for 10 minutes before serving.

Note: The best accompaniment to this dish is simply creamed potatoes.

The Hour Before

Jerusalem Scallops

8 small scallops	(24)
2 Jerusalem artichokes	(6)
2 tomatoes	(6)
1 dessertspoon chopped green pepper	(2)
1 oz. butter	(3)
1 dessertspoon flour	(3)
$\frac{1}{3}$ pint milk	(1)
2 tablespoons grated mild English cheese	(6)
seasoning	

Preparation

Peel and slice the tomatoes. Wash, deseed and very finely chop the green pepper. Scrape the artichokes, and cook in boiling salted water for 10 minutes. Drain and slice. Grate the cheese. Wash and drain the scallops.

Action

1. Make a sauce with the butter, flour, milk and seasoning. After the sauce has simmered for 4 minutes, withdraw the pan from the heat and stir in the grated cheese and adjust the seasoning.

2. **Butter** a casserole and put in the scallops with equal sized pieces of the artichokes and tomatoes and sprinkle over the finely-chopped green pepper. Cover with the cheese sauce.

3. **Cook** in a moderate oven for 40 minutes.

The Day Before

Three Fish Casserole

4 oz. of ready-cooked lobster or crab	(¾ lb.)
2 oz. cooked peeled prawns	(6)
8 oz. halibut steak	(1½ lb.)
2 oz. mushrooms	(4)
2 small tomatoes	(6)
2 oz. butter	(3½)
1½ oz. flour	(2½)
2 tablespoons sherry	(5)
1 onion	(1)
1 carrot	(1)
¾ pint chicken stock	(1¼)
1 bay leaf	(1)
1 small clove garlic	(1)
1 pinch dried tarragon	(1)
1 pinch cayenne	(1)
seasoning	

Preparation

Skin and chop onion(s), garlic, carrot(s), tomatoes and mushrooms.

Action

1. **Put** the stock, the onion(s), carrot(s), garlic, bay leaf, tarragon, cayenne and seasoning in a saucepan and bring it to the boil. Simmer for 10 minutes, then add the halibut and continue to

cook gently for 7 minutes. Remove the fish from the pan and
bone it. Put the bones back into the pan with the stock, cover
the pan and simmer for another 10 minutes. Then strain the
liquid into a jug.

2. Place the halibut in a casserole with the tomatoes and while
   the stock is simmering sauté the mushrooms in ½ (1) oz. of
   the butter, then add these to the fish and tomatoes.

3. When the stock has been strained, make a sauce with the rest
   of the butter, the flour and ½ (1) pint of the stock. When the
   sauce has simmered for 4 minutes, withdraw from the heat,
   stir in the sherry and adjust the seasoning. Pour it over the
   fish, allow to cool and chill in refrigerator overnight.

Next Day

Put the dish in a low oven to reheat, and when the sauce has
become liquid, stir in the crab or lobster and the prawns, and return to the oven until thoroughly heated.

The Day Before

Prawn Curry

1 small tin Le-Ka-Ri mild Malayan curry sauce   (1 large)
8 oz. cooked peeled prawns   (1½ lb.)

Serve with boiled rice, fried popadoms and Bombay duck
(bought from Indian and delicatessen stores), and side dishes
of:

   dried chillies
   sliced tomatoes and onions
   sliced bananas
   sliced pineapple
   sliced green peppers
   toasted almonds
   coconut (shredded or desiccated)
   various chutneys

Preparation

Peel and slice the onion and tomato and put them in an airtight
container in the refrigerator until required. Slice the green pepper
and deseed, then put this in a separate container in the refrigerator. Soak the Bombay ducks in water overnight.

Action

Open the tin of curry sauce and tip it into a casserole. Add the
prawns, cover the dish and leave it in the refrigerator overnight
to absorb the flavour of the curry.

Next Day

Heat the casserole in a low oven. Boil the rice in salt water for
13 minutes then tip it into a sieve and run boiling water through
it to separate the grains. Drain and put it in a covered dish in a
low oven to keep warm until you are ready to eat. Arrange the
ingredients you are having as side dishes in individual bowls.
Drain and dry the Bombay ducks, and fry them, and the popadoms, in deep very hot fat until they are crisp. (See footnote p. 90.)

The Day Before

Prawns with Tomatoes and Mushrooms

8 oz. cooked peeled prawns	($1\frac{1}{2}$ lb.)
4 oz. mushrooms	($\frac{3}{4}$ lb.)
1 onion	(2)
$\frac{1}{2}$ small green pepper	(1)
2 fresh tomatoes	(6)
2 oz. butter	(4)
$\frac{1}{2}$ tin condensed tomato soup	(1)
1 small clove garlic	(2)
1 bay leaf	(2)
2 sprigs parsley	(4)
1 sprig thyme	(1)
1 clove	(2)
1 pinch paprika	($\frac{1}{4}$ teaspoon)
seasoning	

Preparation

Wash and slice the mushrooms. Peel and chop tomatoes and onion(s). Finely chop green pepper and garlic. Tie together the bay leaf, parsley, cloves and thyme.

Action

1. In a heavy saucepan heat the butter and sauté the mushrooms, onion(s), green pepper and garlic, and cook over a low heat for 10 minutes.

2. To the contents of the saucepan add the tomato soup, fresh tomatoes, the herbs, paprika and seasoning. Cover the pan then simmer for 20 minutes, stirring occasionally.

3. Transfer the contents of the pan to a casserole and extract the herbs. Allow to cool, and store overnight in the refrigerator.

Next Day

Stir in the peeled prawns, then reheat the dish in a low oven.

Note: This dish is best when served with boiled rice and a tossed green salad.

The Day Before

Green Pea Prawns

1 large cup cooked peeled prawns	(3)
1 large cup cooked green peas	(3)
1 oz. butter	(3)
1 dessertspoon flour	(3)
1 large cup milk	(3)
2 tablespoons sherry	(6)
seasoning	

Preparation

Shell the peas if not using frozen ones.

Action

1. Boil the peas in a little salted water in the ordinary way.

2. Make a sauce with the butter, flour and milk. When the sauce
   has boiled for 2 minutes, withdraw the pan from the heat and
   stir in the sherry and seasoning.

3. Strain the peas and put them in a casserole with the prawns and
   pour the sauce over the top. Allow to cool, and store in refrigerator overnight.

Next Day

Reheat thoroughly in a low oven.

The Day Before

Scampi Risotto

½ lb. fresh or frozen cooked peeled scampi	(1½)
½ cup tinned tomatoes	(1 8-oz. tin)
6 stuffed olives	(12)
1 teaspoon capers	(2)
½ cup uncooked rice	(1½)
2 tablespoons oil	(6)
1 cup chicken stock	(3)
1 wine glass white wine	(2½)
1 dessertspoon chopped parsley	(3)
seasoning	

Preparation

Wash the rice. Slice the olives and capers and put in airtight containers in the refrigerator for use the following day.

Action

1. Heat the oil in a heavy frying-pan and sauté the scampi for 5
   minutes, then transfer them to a large heavy saucepan.

2. To the remains of the oil in the frying-pan add the rice, and fry until brown, stirring regularly. Then add this to the scampi.

3. To the ingredients in the saucepan add the tomatoes, stock, wine and seasoning. Cover the pan and cook over a very low heat until the rice is soft and all the liquid has been absorbed, stirring occasionally. Transfer to a casserole. Allow to cool, and chill overnight in the refrigerator.

Next Day

Stir in the capers and sliced olives and reheat the dish thoroughly in a low oven. While the dish is heating, chop the parsley and at the point of service sprinkle it over the top.

General Notes on Choosing Poultry and Game

When the birds are young, their legs should be smooth and pliable, with fine scales, and in the case of the male bird, their spurs should only just be developing. Other bones, such as the beak and feet should also be supple. When selecting birds before they are plucked, their eyes should be bright, they should still have a certain amount of down under their wings and breast, and the wing feathers should pull out easily. If the birds have already been plucked, the skin should be unwrinkled and the breast plump and firm.

	Season	*Cooking Time*	
Chicken	All year ⎱	Approx. 20 min. per lb. A little less	
Domestic Duck		for very young small birds.	
Grouse	12th Aug.–10th Dec.	25–30 min. ⎤	These times are for
Partridges	1st Sept.–1st Feb.	20–25 min.	young birds. Old
Pheasants	15th Oct.–1st Feb.	50–60 min.	birds require slower
Pigeons	All year	25–35 min. ⎦	cooking.

The Hour Before

Bundled Chicken

2 portions of chicken breast	(6)
1 wing of chicken	(3)
2 small tomatoes	(6)
⅓ green pepper	(1)
3 rashers bacon	(9)
3 tablespoons fresh white breadcrumbs	(9)
1 egg	(2)
2 tablespoons oil	(6)
1½ oz. butter	(4)
1 tablespoon flour	(3)
1 small clove garlic	(1 large)
1 pinch basil	(½ teaspoon)
seasoning	

Preparation

If you cannot get your butcher to do it for you, cut the chicken breast from the bone with a sharp boning knife, and remove the skin as carefully as possible and reserve. Beat the breast(s) until they become very thin. Cut the flesh from the wing(s) into small pieces. Cut the rinds off the bacon. Skin and chop the tomatoes. Wash, deseed and finely chop the green pepper. Make the breadcrumbs.

Action

1. Crisply fry 2 (6) rashers of the bacon, saving the other 1 (3). When the bacon is crisp take it from the pan and crumble it very finely. Mix the crushed bacon with the breadcrumbs.

2. Add 1 (2) tablespoons of the oil to the bacon fat and lightly sauté the pieces of chicken wing with the tomatoes, green pepper, garlic (which you should crush), basil and seasoning.

3. Spread the mixture from the frying-pan on the chicken breasts. Roll them up and tie them round with the skin you have reserved.

4. Roll the bundles in the flour. Then break the egg(s) into a bowl and beat lightly. Dip the floured bundles in this and then roll them in the mixture of breadcrumbs and bacon.

5. Add the rest of the oil and the butter to the frying-pan and cook the bundles for 10 minutes, turning to brown on all sides.

6. Transfer the bundles to a heatproof dish and cover with the other rasher(s) of bacon. Cook in a moderate oven for 20 minutes.

Note: If you will be in a hurry 'the hour before', you can make this dish up to the end of number 4 the day before, and store in the refrigerator.

The Day Before

Chieveley Chicken

2 portions of chicken	(1 large chicken)
1 medium onion	(3)
2 tomatoes	(6)
2 oz. button mushrooms	(6)
1 tablespoon oil	(3)
1½ oz. butter	(3)
½ small tin condensed tomato soup	(1)
4 tablespoons white wine	(1 wine glass)
½ cup chicken stock	(1½)
2 tablespoons single cream	(¼ pint)
1 bay leaf	(2)
½ clove garlic	(1)
1 small sprig or pinch of thyme	(1)
1 small sprig or pinch of marjoram	(1)
seasoning	

Preparation

Cut the chicken into 2 (6) serving joints (most butchers will do this for you). Peel and chop the onion(s) and tomatoes. Wash the mushrooms. Peel and finely chop garlic.

Action

1. Heat the butter and oil in a large heavy saucepan and fry the onion(s) until soft.

2. Add the chicken pieces to the onion(s) and brown.

3. Add the stock, wine, tomato soup, tomatoes, mushrooms, herbs, garlic and seasoning. Bring to the boil gently, then transfer the contents of the saucepan to a casserole and cook in a moderate oven for 45 minutes. When cooked, remove casserole from oven, extract bay leaf and the herbs if you were able to use fresh ones, and allow to cool. Chill in the refrigerator overnight.

Next Day

Reheat casserole in a low oven and at the point of service stir in the cream.

The Day Before

Chin Chin Chicken

2 portions of chicken	(1 whole chicken)
2 onions	(5)
1 stick of celery	(3)
½ green pepper	(1)
2 oz. mushrooms	(4)
6 stuffed green olives	(18)
½ cup tinned pineapple	(1½)
2 oz. mild English cheese	(4)
1 tablespoon oil	(3)
1 oz. butter	(3)
2 tablespoons sherry	(6)
1 teaspoon curry powder	(3)
seasoning	

87

Preparation

If using a whole chicken cut it into serving-sized joints. Slice and
chop onions, mushrooms, pepper, celery and olives. Cut the
pineapple into cubes and grate cheese.

Action

1. Heat the butter and oil in a heavy frying-pan and brown the
   chicken joints. Transfer them to a casserole.
2. In the remainder of the fat, sauté the onion, celery, pepper and
   mushrooms. Add the curry powder and cook for 10 minutes.
3. Transfer the contents of the frying-pan to the casserole with
   the chicken and add the pineapple, olives and sherry. Cover
   the casserole and cook in a moderate oven for 50 minutes.
   Remove from oven, allow to cool, and chill in refrigerator
   overnight.

Next Day

Sprinkle the grated cheese over the casserole and reheat in a low
oven.

The Day Before
Chicken Curry

2 chicken joints	(1 whole chicken)
1 dessertspoon desiccated coconut	(2)
$\frac{1}{2}$ pint chicken stock	($1\frac{1}{2}$)
$1\frac{1}{2}$ oz. butter	(4)
1 small cooking-apple	(1 large)
1 onion	(3)
1 dessertspoon sultanas	(3)
1 large tomato	(3)
1 teaspoon brown sugar	(1 dessertspoon)
1 dessertspoon lemon juice	(3)
1 dessertspoon chutney	(2)
1 teaspoon curry powder	(3)
1 teaspoon curry paste	(3)

Serve with boiled rice, fried popadoms (bought from
Indian and delicatessen stores), and Bombay duck,
and side dishes of, perhaps:

dried chillies
sliced tomatoes and onions
sliced bananas
sliced green peppers
sliced pineapple
toasted almonds or peanuts
various chutneys
sliced cucumber in French dressing
desiccated coconut

Preparation

Bring the stock to the boil and add the desiccated coconut and
leave it to soak for at least half an hour. Peel, core and slice the
apple. Peel and slice onion(s) and tomato(es). Squeeze lemon
juice. Soak the Bombay ducks in water overnight. Prepare any
of the side dishes recommended above and store the ingredients
in separate airtight containers in the refrigerator.

Action

1. Melt the butter in a large heavy frying-pan and sauté the apple
   and onion(s) for five minutes, then extract and keep on one
   side.

2. Add the chicken and brown thoroughly.

3. Stir in the curry powder and paste, and cook for 2 minutes.
   Blend in the stock, which you should strain to discard the
   coconut. Bring to the boil.

4. Add all the other ingredients, cover the pan and simmer for
   40 (60) minutes or until the chicken is tender.

5. When the chicken is cooked, remove it from the pan and cut
   into pieces discarding the bones and skin. Put in a casserole
   and pour the sauce over it. Cool, and chill overnight in the
   refrigerator.

Next Day

Heat the casserole in a moderate oven. Arrange the ingredients you are having as side dishes in individual bowls.[1] Boil the rice in salt water for 13 minutes, then tip into a sieve and run boiling water through it to separate the grains. Drain the Bombay ducks and pat dry. Fry them and the popadoms in deep very hot fat until crisp.

The Hour Before

Colonel's Nostalgia

2 chicken portions	(6)
1 large onion	(3)
1½ oz. butter	(3)
1 tablespoon oil	(3)
2 tablespoons brandy	(5)
¼ pint double cream	(½)
1 teaspoon curry powder	(3)
seasoning	

Preparation

Skin and slice onion(s).

Action

1. Heat the butter and oil in a heavy saucepan and sauté the onion(s) with the lid of the pan on for 10 minutes, stirring occasionally.

2. Add the pieces of chicken. Cover the pan again and cook for 30 minutes over a gentle heat, turning the chicken occasionally.

[1] From here these things can be done the day before if you are going to be rushed the next day. If you do them in advance, next day butter a casserole and put the rice in it with a knob or two of butter on it, and heat in a very low oven. The popadoms and Bombay ducks should be laid on a baking-tray and be crisped in the oven.

3. After 30 minutes, stir in the curry powder and seasoning. Cook for 5 more minutes, then remove from the heat and stir in the brandy and cream. Transfer to a casserole and keep in a very low oven until you are ready to eat.

Note: If you have to be out in the kitchen doing something else, you can leave the chicken at stage 2, and then 10 minutes or so before eating, heat the chicken again in the saucepan and stir in the curry, brandy and cream and serve it immediately.
This is a very rich dish and is best served with plain vegetables, such as courgettes, mange-tout peas, spinach or French beans.

The Day Before

Orchard Chicken

2 portions of chicken	(1 large chicken)
12 black cherries—fresh or tinned	(30)
1 oz. butter	(3)
1 dessertspoon flour	(3)
¾ cup milk	(2)
2 tablespoons sherry	(6)
2 oz. mild English cheese	(4)
1 small onion	(2)
2 black peppercorns	(4)
1 bay leaf	(2)
1 pinch thyme	(1)
1 pinch marjoram	(1)
seasoning	

Preparation

Skin and cut the onion(s) in half. Grate the cheese. If you are using fresh cherries, or unpitted ones, stone them. To save time, we recommend you use the tinned black pitted cherries, which in this case are as good, unless you happen to be making this dish at the height of the cherry season.

Action

1. Put the chicken in a saucepan with sufficient water to cover, with the onion(s), bay leaf, marjoram, thyme, peppercorns and salt. Simmer for approximately 40 minutes or until the flesh can be taken off the bones.

2. When the chicken is cooked, strain the stock into a jug. Remove the chicken from the saucepan, take off the skin and bone. Put the chicken pieces in a shallow heatproof dish and arrange the cherries on top.

3. Make a sauce with the butter, flour, milk and 1½ (2) cups of the stock. When the sauce has boiled for 2 minutes, withdraw the pan from the heat and stir in the sherry and grated cheese. Adjust seasoning.

4. Pour the sauce over the chicken and cherries. Allow to cool, and chill in the refrigerator overnight.

Next Day
Reheat in a low oven.

The Day Before
Chicken Mousse

2 chicken joints	(1 medium chicken)
1 egg	(3)
1 onion	(1)
1 carrot	(1)
⅓ packet of aspic	(1)
1½ oz. butter	(3)
1 dessertspoon flour	(3)
½ cup milk	(1½)
2 tablespoons white wine	(6)
2 tablespoons double cream	(¼ pint)
1 clove	(2)
1 bay leaf	(2)
1 sprig thyme	(1)
seasoning	

Preparation

Peel the onion and carrot and cut in half. Stick the cloves in the onion. Separate the egg white(s) and yolk(s).

Action

1. Put the chicken in a saucepan with the onion, cloves, carrot, bay leaf, thyme, seasoning and sufficient water to cover. Bring to the boil then simmer for 35 (60) minutes.

2. When the chicken is cooked, strain the stock into a jug, and whilst the chicken cools sufficiently to handle, make up the aspic, following the directions on the packet, using $\frac{1}{4}$ ($\frac{1}{2}$) pint of the stock as the liquid. Skin and bone the chicken and mince finely.

3. Make a sauce with the butter, flour, the milk, and an equal quantity of the chicken stock. When the sauce has simmered for 4 minutes, withdraw the pan from the heat and pour a small quantity of it on to the egg yolk(s) and mix before returning to the pan. Stir in the wine and season.

4. When the sauce has cooled, stir in the cream and two-thirds of the aspic, saving enough with which to glaze the top of the mousse. Then if you have a mixer, put the chicken and sauce into it and blend to a smooth consistency. If not, blend as smoothly as possible by hand. Adjust seasoning.

5. Whisk the egg white(s) until stiff and fold them into the chicken mixture. Pour into a soufflé dish and allow to get completely cold.

6. Garnish with perhaps a flower cut out of slices of tomato, using cucumber skin for the leaves and stalks, and spoon over the remains of the aspic. The aspic is ready when it is just beginning to set. Chill in refrigerator until required.

The Day Before

Olive Chicken

4 chicken thighs	(12)
2 oz. large black olives	(6)
2 medium onions	(5)
½ small green pepper	(1)
1 tablespoon oil	(3)
1½ oz. butter	(3)
2 tablespoons port	(6)
1½ cups chicken stock	(4)
1 pinch dried thyme	(1)
seasoning	
seasoned flour	

Preparation

Peel and slice onions. Wash, deseed and slice green pepper. Stone the olives. Prepare the seasoned flour, adding the pinch of dried thyme.

Action

1. Heat the butter and oil in a frying-pan and sauté the onions for 7 minutes, then transfer them to a casserole. Meanwhile, toss your chicken joints in the seasoned flour.

2. In the remains of the fat in the pan, fry the chicken pieces for 10 minutes, or until the outside is golden.

3. Add the stoned olives and green pepper, and blend in the port, stock and seasoning. Transfer the contents of the frying-pan to the casserole with the onions. Cover and cook in a moderate oven for 30 minutes. Remove from oven, allow to cool, then chill in the refrigerator overnight.

Next Day

Reheat the casserole in a moderate oven.

The Day Before

No Ordinary Chicken Pie

2 small chicken joints	(6, or 1 whole chicken)
1 oz. mushrooms	(4)
2 oz. liver pâté	(6)
1 egg yolk	(3)
1½ oz. butter	(3)
½ dessertspoon flour	(1½)
1 tablespoon sherry	(3)
1 clove	(2)
1 pinch thyme	(¼ teaspoon)
1 bay leaf	(2)
seasoning	
3 oz. flaky pastry to cover	(8)

Preparation

Wash and slice the mushrooms. Separate egg white(s) and yolk(s).

Action

1. Put the chicken in a saucepan with sufficient water to cover
   the herbs and seasoning. Simmer for 30 (50 for the whole
   chicken) minutes, or until you can take the flesh off the bones.
   Meanwhile make the pastry, and put it to chill in the refrigerator. (Appendix I).

2. While the chicken is cooking, sauté the mushrooms in ½ (1½) oz.
   of the butter.

3. When the chicken is cooked, strain the stock into a jug. Bone
   the chicken and extract the skin, and cut the flesh into smallish
   pieces and place in a pie-dish.

4. Make a sauce with the rest of the butter, the flour and 1½ (3)
   cups of the stock. When the sauce has boiled for 2 minutes,
   withdraw the pan from the heat and stir in the sherry; then
   tip a little of the stock on to the egg yolk(s), mix thoroughly,
   and when the stock has cooled a little stir in the egg yolk(s),

95

together with the sautéed mushrooms and liver pâté. Adjust the seasoning and pour the sauce over the chicken. Allow to cool and chill overnight in the refrigerator.

Next Day

Roll out the pastry and cover the chicken, then bake in a hot oven for 30 minutes.

The Day Before

Point to Point Chicken

2 portions of chicken breast	(6)
1 onion	(2)
½ teaspoon finely-chopped horseradish	(1½)
1½ oz. butter	(3)
1 dessertspoon flour	(2 heaped)
½ cup milk	(1)
⅛ pint single cream	(⅓)
1 clove	(2)
1 sprig thyme	(1)
1 bay leaf	(2)
seasoning	

Preparation

Finely chop or grate the horseradish. Peel the onion(s) and stick in the clove(s).

Action

1. Simmer the chicken portions over a low heat in a closed saucepan for 45 minutes with sufficient water to cover, with onion(s) and clove(s), thyme, bay leaf, and seasoning.

2. When the chicken is cooked, strain the liquid into a jug and put the pieces of chicken in a casserole.

3. Make a sauce with the butter, flour, milk and 1 (3) cups of the chicken stock. Simmer for 4 minutes. Adjust seasoning and stir in the grated horseradish. Pour the sauce over the chicken and allow it to cool before chilling in the refrigerator overnight.

Next Day

Reheat the dish thoroughly in a low oven, and at the point of service, stir in the cream.

The Hour Before

Popping Chicken

2 chicken joints	(6)
2 oz. melted butter	(4)
1 cup crushed rice crispies	(2)
seasoning	

Preparation

Crush the rice crispies.

Action

1. Melt the butter.
2. Dry the chicken joints and dip them in the melted butter, to which you should add plenty of seasoning.
3. Roll the buttered chicken joints in the crushed rice crispies and lay them well spaced out on a sheet of foil on a shallow baking-tray. If there is any butter and rice crispies left over, sprinkle them on top.
4. Bake in a moderately hot oven for 50 minutes.

The Day Before

Pulled Chicken

2 chicken joints	(1 whole chicken)
2 hard-boiled eggs	(6)
3 rashers bacon	(8)
6 small sweet gherkins	(12)
2 medium-sized potatoes	(6)
1 small onion	(2)
1 carrot	(2)
1–2 tablespoons mayonnaise (see p. 208)	(4–6)
1 tablespoon single cream	(3)
1 bay leaf	(1)
2 peppercorns	(4)
seasoning	

Preparation

Peel and roughly chop onion(s) and carrot(s). Peel the potatoes. Cut the rind from the bacon.

Action

1. Put the chicken in a saucepan with enough water to cover, with onion(s), carrot(s), bay leaf, peppercorns and salt. Simmer for 40 (60) minutes, or until the chicken is tender.

2. While the chicken is cooking boil the potatoes and mash them in the usual way. Hard boil the eggs, peel and chop finely. Fry or grill the bacon and chop finely when crisp. Finely chop the gherkins.

3. When the chicken is cooked, strain off the stock and keep for making soup or something. Allow the chicken to cool, then pull the flesh from the bones, discarding the skin, and shred into strips about 1 in. long.

4. Put the chicken into a mixing-bowl with the other ingredients, using sufficient mayonnaise and cream to bind it all together. Cover, and chill overnight in the refrigerator.

Next Day

Turn the mixture on to a plate, perhaps on a bed of shredded lettuce, and make into an attractive shape which you could garnish with a line of sliced stuffed olives sitting on thinly-sliced peeled cucumber. Store in the refrigerator until required.

The Day Before

Tarragon Chicken

2 chicken joints	(1 large chicken)
1 tablespoon oil	(2)
½ oz. butter	(1½)
1 wineglass white wine	(2½)
1 pinch dried tarragon	(½ teaspoon)
seasoning	
seasoned flour	

Preparation

When using the whole chicken, cut into serving-size joints—most butchers will do this for you. Prepare the seasoned flour, adding the dried tarragon to it.

Action

1. Roll the chicken joints in the seasoned flour so that they are very well coated.

2. Heat the butter and oil in a heavy frying-pan and cook the chicken joints for 10 minutes or until they are lightly browned.

3. Transfer the chicken joints to a casserole, and blend the wine into the juices in the frying-pan and simmer for 10 minutes.

4. Pour the liquid from the frying-pan over the chicken. Season and cook in a moderate oven for 30 minutes. Allow to cool, and chill overnight in refrigerator.

Next Day

Reheat in a moderate oven.

The Day Before

Chicken with Wine

2 portions of chicken	(6, or 1 large chicken)
8 button onions	(20)
2 oz. button mushrooms	(6)
2 rashers bacon	(6)
1 small carrot	(2)
1 stick celery	(2)
1 tablespoon oil	(3)
¾ oz. butter	(2)
1 dessertspoon flour	(2)
2 tablespoons brandy	(6)
1½ glasses red wine	(½ bottle)
½ cup stock	(1½)
½ small clove garlic	(1)
1 pinch thyme	(1)
1 pinch basil	(1)
seasoning	

Preparation

Cut the chicken into serving joints. Peel the onions and garlic.
Wash the mushrooms. Scrub and slice carrot(s) and celery in
halves. Remove the rind from the bacon and dice. Blend the
butter and flour into a paste and put in the refrigerator overnight.

Action

1. Heat the oil in a heavy frying-pan and sauté the onions and
   bacon. When they are lightly coloured remove from the pan
   and put on one side.

100

2. In the remaining oil fry the chicken until it becomes golden (about 10 minutes).

3. Pour the brandy over the chicken pieces in the frying-pan and flame.

4. Return the onions and bacon to the pan and add the mushrooms, wine, stock, thyme, basil, and squeeze in the garlic. Bring to the boil and season.

5. Transfer the contents of the frying-pan to a casserole and arrange the pieces of carrot and celery on top. Cook in a moderate oven for 40 minutes. When cooked remove from the oven and extract the celery and carrot. Allow to cool, and chill overnight in the refrigerator.

Next Day

Reheat the casserole and when it is really hot stir in the blended butter and flour to thicken. Return the dish to the oven and allow it to boil for a few minutes to cook the flour, then turn the oven to very low until you are ready to eat.

The Hour Before

Chicken Livers

½ lb. chicken livers   (1½)
2 oz. mushrooms   (6)
1 medium onion   (2)
2 tablespoons sliced celery   (6)
2 oz. butter   (4)
⅓ cup chicken stock   (1)
4 tablespoons commercially soured cream   (½ pint)
1 dessertspoon lemon juice   (3)
½ teaspoon Worcester sauce   (2)
1 tablespoon chopped parsley   (3)
seasoning
seasoned flour

101

Preparation

Prepare seasoned flour. Peel and slice onion(s). Wash and slice mushrooms and celery. Chop parsley. Squeeze lemon juice.

Action

1. Roll the chicken livers in the seasoned flour.

2. Heat the butter in a large frying-pan and sauté the livers, onion(s), celery and mushrooms for 10 minutes.

3. Add the chicken stock and Worcester sauce. Cover the pan and simmer for a further 10 minutes.

4. Remove from heat and stir in the sour cream and seasoning. Return the pan to the heat and cook over a low heat in a covered pan until the sauce has thickened—this takes about 8 minutes.

5. Transfer to a casserole and keep in a very low oven until you are ready to eat, and at the point of service, stir in the lemon juice and chopped parsley.

Note: A good accompaniment to this dish is boiled rice, spaghetti or noodles.

The Hour Before

De Luxe Duck

2 duck portions	(6)
1½ small oranges	(3)
2 dessertspoons shredded almonds	(6)
1 teaspoon oil	(3)
1 teaspoon salt	(2)
1 tablespoon brandy	(3)
seasoning	

Preparation

Cut any excess fat you can from the duck portions. Grate the peel from ½ (1) orange and squeeze the juice from it. Peel the other 1 (2) orange(s) in the ordinary way, then cut the segments out of their inner skins.

Action

1. Pour the oil into the palm of your hand and rub it into the duck skin. Then pour the salt into your hand and rub that in as well.

2. Place the duck portions, skin side down, in a frying-pan over a very gentle heat, and cook for 5 minutes. By that time quite a lot of fat should have run out of the duck, so turn over the portions and brown the other side in the resulting fat.

3. Drain off all the fat, then flame the duck portions in the brandy.

4. Transfer the contents of the frying-pan to a casserole. Sprinkle on the orange rind, the juice and the almonds, then lay the orange segments on top. Grind a little black pepper over the oranges. Cover the casserole and cook in a low oven for 50 minutes.

Note: In some parts of the country it is possible to buy portions of duck. However, if it is necessary to buy a whole bird, we suggest you curry the remainder, following the recipe for chicken curry if you have *not* already cooked the duck, or as for prawn curry if you have.

The Day Before

Casseroled Grouse

1 elderly grouse	(3)
2 oz. mushrooms	(6)
8 button onions	(15)
2 rashers streaky bacon	(6)
1 small carrot	(3)
3 small tomatoes	(6)
½ oz. butter	(2)
½ dessertspoon flour	(1 tablespoon)
1 wineglass red wine	(3)
½ wineglass water	(1½)
2 tablespoons port	(4)
1 teaspoon lemon juice	(2)
1 sprig thyme	(1)
1 sprig parsley	(1)
seasoning	

Preparation

Skin the onions, tomatoes and carrot(s), and chop the latter two. Chop up the bacon and remove rind. Wash the mushrooms and slice if large, but leave whole if they are the button kind. Tie the parsley and thyme together.

Action

1. In a frying-pan cook the diced bacon until all the fat has come out and the meat is crisp. Remove the bacon from the pan and transfer to a casserole.

2. In the resulting fat brown the grouse all over, adding a little oil if necessary, then transfer them to the casserole.

3. Add the butter to the remains of the bacon fat in the frying-pan and sauté the onions, carrot(s) and mushrooms, sprinkling the latter with the lemon juice. Cook for 7 minutes, then transfer the vegetables to the casserole and add the tomatoes and seasoning.

4. Blend the flour with the remains of the fat in the frying-pan, and slowly stir in the wine, port and water. Bring the sauce to the boil and cook for 2 minutes, then pour it over the grouse. Add the parsley and thyme and cook in a very low oven for 2 hours. When cooked, remove from oven and extract the herbs. Allow to cool, and chill overnight in the refrigerator.

Next Day

Cut the birds in half, put them in a clean casserole with the other ingredients, and reheat in a low oven.

Note: This is a good way of cooking elderly partridge as well, though young ones are best roasted.

The Hour Before

Pheasant with Cream

1 small hen pheasant	(2)
8 button onions	(24)
2 oz. button mushrooms	($\frac{1}{2}$ lb.)
4 oz. butter	(8)
2 tablespoons single cream	($\frac{1}{4}$ pint)
seasoning	

Preparation

Peel button onions. Wash button mushrooms.

Action

1. Heat the butter in a heavy frying-pan and sauté the onions for 10 minutes. Transfer to a casserole.

2. Brown the pheasant(s) in the butter and put in the casserole with the onions. Add the mushrooms, the butter from the frying-pan, and seasoning. Cover and cook in a moderately hot oven for 1 hour.

105

3. At the point of service stir in the cream. To serve, transfer the pheasant(s) to a serving-plate and surround with the other ingredients, or serve them in a separate dish if you don't have a large enough plate.

Note: One pheasant is fairly extravagant for two, but you can devil the legs next day. To do this you make deep incisions in the flesh and into them rub a mixture of Worcester sauce, French mustard and cayenne pepper, made to suit your own taste. Brush the meat with butter or oil and cook quickly under the grill. But only do this with a reasonably young bird.

The Day Before

Casseroled Pigeon

2 pigeons	(6)
1 rasher bacon	(3)
1 small tin water chestnuts	(2)
8 button onions	(24)
1 tablespoon oil	(3)
¾ oz. butter	(2)
1 dessertspoon flour	(2 tablespoons)
1 glass red wine	(2)
1½ cups stock	(3½)
2 tablespoons port	(6)
1 dessertspoon bramble jelly	(3)
1 bay leaf	(3)
1 sprig thyme	(2)
1 dessertspoon chopped parsley	(3)
seasoning	

Preparation

Cut the rinds from the bacon and dice the meat. Skin the onions.

Action

1. Put the bacon in a frying-pan and cook until crisp, then transfer to a casserole. (A very large one will be needed for 6.)

106

2. Add the oil to the bacon fat and sauté the button onions for five minutes, shaking the pan occasionally. Then transfer them to the casserole.

3. Brown the pigeons in the remaining fat, then transfer them to the casserole and add the water chestnuts, wine, stock, bay leaf, thyme and seasoning. Cover the dish and cook in a very low oven for 1½ hours.

4. When the birds are cooked, strain the juice into a jug, and transfer the bacon, onions and water chestnuts to a fresh casserole. Carve the breasts from the pigeons and put this with the onions, etc.

5. In a saucepan heat the butter and stir in the flour. Cook the roux for 2 minutes, stirring constantly, then withdraw from the heat and blend in the juice in which the pigeon was cooked. Return it to the heat again and bring to the boil, then stir in the port and bramble jelly and pour the sauce over the pigeons. Allow to cool, and store overnight in the refrigerator.

Next Day

Reheat the casserole in a low oven. Meanwhile chop the parsley and sprinkle it on at the point of service.

Note: This is also an extremely good way of cooking pheasant. If you are feeling hungry and extravagant, two people can eat a small hen pheasant, and two would serve six.
If you are living in the country you may have difficulty in getting water chestnuts, which are Chinese and quite unlike ordinary sweet chestnuts, but a lot of delicatessen shops do stock them.

General Notes on Choosing Meat

Ham and Bacon Joints

The meat should be deep pink and be firm to the touch with white fat on the outside, but not too much running through it. The biggest pitfall in buying a ham or bacon joint is that it will be too salt. Unfortunately there is no way of telling this and it is therefore a sensible precaution to soak the meat in cold water overnight before cooking.

Average time needed for boiling is 25 minutes per pound.

Pork

The best pork to buy is small pork and the meat should be close grained, firm and very pale pink. There should be a layer of white fat covered by a thin smooth rind.

Average time needed for roasting is 30–35 minutes per pound.

Beef

Good beef should be firm to the touch. The flesh should be a deep red colour, but not too dark, and have small veins of fat running through it.

Average time needed for roasting is 20 minutes per pound.

Lamb

Lamb should have a similar appearance to beef, having a strong red colour with small veins of fat running through it and be firm to the touch.

Average time needed for roasting is 20 minutes to the pound, plus 20 minutes over.

Veal

Veal, being very young meat, should be a very delicate shade of pink and have almost no fat.

Average time needed for roasting is 20–25 minutes per pound.

Liver, Kidney, Tongue and Sweetbreads

Unlike other meats, offal should not be hung, but eaten very fresh, and insist on this when you go to your butcher.

The Day Before

Bacon Mousse

6 oz. piece of raw smoked bacon	(1½)
1 teaspoon grated raw onion	(3)
1 tablespoon minced raw celery	(3)
1 tablespoon minced green pepper	(3)
1 tablespoon minced red pepper	(3)
1 small egg	(3)
¾ teaspoon powdered gelatin	(2)
¾ cup well-seasoned chicken stock	(2)
3 tablespoons double cream	(¼ pint)
¼ teaspoon dry mustard	(¾)
1 teaspoon minced parsley	(3)
seasoning	

Fill the centre of the mousse either with home-made mayonnaise (see p. 208), or a mixture of the following:

¼ lb. soft cream cheese	(¾)
1 dessertspoon tomato ketchup	(3)
1 teaspoon Worcester sauce	(3)

Preparation

Mince the bacon. Wash, deseed and mince green and red pepper. Peel and mince celery and onion. Finely chop or mince parsley. Hard boil egg, peel and chop.

Action

1. Soak the gelatin in a little of the stock and bring the remainder of the stock to boiling point. Pour it into a bowl and allow to cool a little, then stir in the gelatin until completely dissolved.

2. Add the grated onion and parsley to the stock, then put the bowl to cool until the gelatin begins to set. (You can speed this up by standing it in a bowl of iced water and it will take about 20 (30) minutes.)

3. While the gelatin is setting, whip the cream and make the mixture for the centre of the mousse. We think the cream

109

cheese centre is best, and all you have to do is combine the cheese, tomato ketchup and Worcester sauce and season to taste.

4. When the stock is beginning to set add the minced bacon, celery, green and red pepper, egg(s) and mustard. Mix it all thoroughly and season with paprika, salt and pepper.

5. Fold in the whipped cream.

6. Pour the mixture into a wet round border mould if available. Otherwise pour into a small (large) soufflé dish, with an upturned egg-cup or similar in the middle to make a hole for the cream cheese or mayonnaise.

7. Chill overnight in the refrigerator. Also chill the filling in a separate covered dish.

Next Day

Turn the mousse out on to a plate. It should turn out quite easily, but if you have trouble, slip a palette knife round the edges to loosen, and stand the dish in a bowl of warm water for about 30 seconds. Garnish with chopped radishes, watercress, etc. and sprinkle a little paprika over the filling, which you should put in the hole in the middle just before serving.

Note: This is a very good summer buffet party dish.

The Hour Before

Blushing Gammon

1 small bacon joint (1 lb. approx.)	(2 lb. approx.)
2 onions	(3)
1 carrot	(1)
2 large tomatoes	(6)
¼ pint white wine	(¾)
3 tablespoons single cream	(⅓ pint)
1 bay leaf	(2)
2 black peppercorns	(4)
1 eggspoon dried tarragon	(2)
seasoning	

Preparation

Skin and chop 1 (2) of the onions and just skin the other one.
Skin the tomatoes. Soak the bacon joint (overnight if possible),
but anyhow for 2 hours, to get rid of the excess salt. Scrape the
carrot and cut in half.

Action

1. When the bacon has soaked, put it in a large saucepan with
   the whole onion, carrot, bay leaf, peppercorns and sufficient
   water to cover. Simmer over a low heat in a covered pan until
   the meat is cooked. (Allow approximately 20 minutes per
   pound, plus 20 minutes over.)

2. While the meat is cooking, in a separate saucepan stew the
   chopped onion(s) and tarragon with the white wine for 15
   minutes, then add the tomatoes and cook for a further 7
   minutes. Season.

3. Remove the sauce from the heat and if you have an electric
   blender put it in there and mix until smooth. If not, sieve it.
   Return the sauce to the pan until you are ready to eat, when
   you should reheat it, adjust the seasoning and stir in the
   cream. Drain the bacon and serve the sauce separately.

Note: There is no reason why the sauce should not be made the
day before, up to the point where you stir in the cream, then
stored overnight in the refrigerator.

The Day Before

Ham Cream

6 oz. cooked ham	(1¼ lb.)
1 egg	(3)
1 oz. butter	(2½)
1 dessertspoon flour	(3)
⅓ pint milk	(¾)
3 tablespoons double cream	(¼ pint)
2 dessertspoons cold consommé	(6)
1 teaspoon capers	(3)
¼ teaspoon French mustard	(1)
¼ clove crushed garlic	(1 small)
¼ teaspoon Worcester sauce	(1)
black pepper	

Preparation

Mince the ham as finely as possible. Chop the capers. Separate egg yolks and whites.

Action

1. Make a white sauce with the butter, milk and flour. Boil for 4 minutes, then remove from heat and beat in the ham. Then stir in the consommé, egg yolk and cream. Mix thoroughly and season with black pepper, Worcester sauce, French mustard, finely chopped capers and garlic.

2. If you have an electric food-mixer, turn the mixture into the bowl and mix to a smooth consistency. If not, mix it as smoothly as possible by hand.

3. Stiffly beat the egg white(s) and when the mixture is smooth, fold in.

4. Turn the mixture into a soufflé dish and put in the refrigerator to set.

Next Day

Garnish as required. Do not remove from refrigerator too soon,
as the consommé may dissolve and make the cream too runny.
Suggested garnish: Flowers cut out of slices of tomato, using
cucumber peel for the leaves and stalks.

The Hour Before

Gingered Ham

2 $\frac{1}{2}$–$\frac{3}{4}$-inch thick gammon or ham steaks	(6)
$\frac{1}{2}$ cup mixed black and white grapes	(1$\frac{1}{2}$)
$\frac{3}{4}$ oz. butter	(2)
1 tablespoon brown sugar	(3)
1 wineglass red wine	(2)
1 pinch ground ginger	($\frac{1}{2}$ teaspoon)
seasoning	

Preparation

Trim the gammon steaks. Peel and pip the grapes.

Action

1. Heat the butter in a frying-pan and stir in the sugar. Continue
   cooking, stirring constantly until the sugar has dissolved.

2. Add the ham to the frying-pan and cook it for 3 minutes on
   each side.

3. Transfer the contents of the frying-pan to a shallow baking-
   dish. Pour over the wine and sprinkle on the ginger and seasoning.

4. Bake in a moderate oven for 15 minutes, then add the grapes
   and cook at the same temperature for another 10 minutes. At
   this stage you can turn the oven right down so that the ham
   will keep warm until you want to eat it.

The Day Before

Hurried Ham

4 slices of cooked ham	(12)
1 small tin of celery hearts	(1 large)
1 oz. grated strong English cheese	(3)
1 oz. butter	(2½)
1 dessertspoon flour	(2)
⅓ pint milk	(1)
seasoning	

Preparation

Grate the cheese. Trim any excess fat from the ham.

Action

1. Wrap the celery in the slices of ham and place them in an ovenproof dish.

2. Make a sauce with the butter, flour and milk. When the sauce has boiled for 2 minutes, withdraw the saucepan from the heat and stir in the cheese. Season.

3. Pour the sauce over the ham, allow to cool, and chill overnight in the refrigerator.

Next Day

Reheat in a hot oven for 20 minutes.

Note: A successful dish can also be made by substituting asparagus, bananas or endive for the celery. In the case of the latter, an extra ten minutes' cooking will be necessary.

The Hour Before

Banapple Pork

2 4-oz. slices of pork fillet	(6)
1 onion	(3)
1 banana	(3)
1 small cooking-apple	(2 medium)
1½ oz. butter	(3)
1½ cups stock	(3)
seasoning	
seasoned flour	

Preparation

Peel and slice the onion and banana. Skin and core the apple, and cut it into circles. Make the seasoned flour.

Action

1. Roll the pork fillets in the seasoned flour.

2. Heat the butter in a frying-pan and toss the banana in it for 2 minutes. Remove from the pan and place in a casserole.

3. In the remainder of the butter, lightly fry the onions and brown the meat on both sides. Blend in the stock and seasoning and transfer the contents of the frying-pan to the casserole.

4. Arrange the sliced apple circles on top of the pork. Cover the dish and cook in a low oven for 50 minutes.

Note: This dish tends to be a bit colourless, so it is a good idea to garnish it with strips of red pepper and stuffed green olives.

The Hour Before

Field Chops

2 pork chops	(6)
2 oz. mushrooms	(6)
4 tablespoons commercially soured cream	(¼ pint)
1 level dessertspoon sugar	(2)
1 dessertspoon lemon juice	(2)
½ cup water	(1½)
1 pinch thyme	(½ teaspoon)
seasoning	
seasoned flour	

Preparation

Trim the pork chops and render down the surplus fat. Wash and slice the mushrooms. Make the seasoned flour.

Action

1. Sauté the mushrooms in a frying-pan with the rendered-down pork fat. When cooked, transfer to a casserole.

2. Roll the chops in the seasoned flour and sauté them for 3 minutes on each side in the remains of the fat in the pan, adding a little oil if necessary.

3. Put the chops in the casserole with the mushrooms, sour cream, thyme, lemon juice, sugar, seasoning and water. Cover and cook in a moderate oven for 45 minutes.

Note: The casserole should be only just large enough for all the ingredients, otherwise it will be rather dry. If you try to counteract this by adding extra water, you will get too much sauce at the end.

The Hour Before

Nutty Chops

2 pork chops	(6)
2 dessertspoons peanuts	(6)
2 sticks celery	(6)
4 medium-sized tomatoes	(12)
1 small onion	(2)
½ cup stock	(1½)
½ glass white wine	(1)
seasoning	

Preparation

Scrape the celery and chop finely. Peel the onion and chop very finely. Peel and slice tomatoes.

Action

1. Place the chops in a frying-pan over a low heat until the fat begins to come out, then brown them on both sides.

2. While the chops are browning mix together the peanuts, celery, tomatoes and onion, and season.

3. Spread half the vegetables on the bottom of a small (medium) sized casserole.

4. When the chops are browned, place them on the bed of vegetables. Pour over the wine and stock, and spread the rest of the vegetables on top.

5. Cover the casserole and cook in a moderate oven for 1 hour.

The Day Before

Oricot Chops

2 pork chops		(6)
½ small tin apricots	(1 large tin)	
1 small orange		(3)
1 small onion		(3)
1 dessertspoon oil		(2)
1 bay leaf		(1)
seasoning		

Preparation

Peel the onions and chop. Strain the apricots and purée in a liquidizer if available. If not push them through a coarse sieve. Grate the rind from 1 (2) orange(s) very finely. Keep the whole orange(s) until the next day.

Action

1. Heat the oil in a frying-pan and brown the chops for five minutes on each side, then turn them on their backs to crisp the fat. Remove from frying-pan and transfer to casserole.

2. Sauté the onions in the remainder of the fat for 7 minutes, then add them to the casserole.

3. Cover the chops with the apricot purée, orange rind, bay leaf and seasoning. Cook in a moderate oven for 40 minutes. When cooked remove from oven, cool, and chill overnight in the refrigerator.

Next Day

Reheat the casserole in a moderate oven. Meanwhile skin and slice the orange with which you should garnish the dish at the point of service.

The Day Before

Pork with Tomatoes

2 pork chops	(6)
2 oz. mushrooms	(6)
1 onion	(2)
½ green pepper	(1)
2 fresh tomatoes	(6)
1 oz. butter	(2)
½ tin condensed tomato soup	(1)
1 clove garlic	(1)
1 bay leaf	(1)
1 pinch thyme	(½ teaspoon)
1 pinch paprika	(¼ teaspoon)
seasoning.	

Preparation

Wash and slice mushrooms. Peel and chop tomatoes and onions. Deseed green pepper then finely chop it and the garlic.

Action

1. In a large heavy frying-pan heat the butter and brown the chops for 5 minutes on each side, then transfer to a casserole.

2. In the remains of the fat sauté the mushrooms, onion, garlic and green pepper for 7–10 minutes, stirring occasionally.

3. To the frying-pan add the tomato soup, fresh tomatoes, bay leaf, thyme, paprika and seasoning. Cover the frying-pan with a lid and simmer the contents for 10 minutes.

4. Pour the contents of the frying-pan over the chops and cover the casserole and cook in a low oven for 30 minutes. Remove from the oven, allow to cool, and chill overnight in the refrigerator.

Next Day

Reheat casserole in a moderate oven.

The Hour Before

Plum Pork

2 4-oz. slices of pork fillet	(6)
3 large fresh plums	(9)
1 tablespoon sugar	(3)
1 glass red wine	(2)
1 clove	(2)
2 tablespoons oil	(4)
seasoning	

Preparation

Nil, unless you like to prepare the plums in advance. They need stewing until soft with the sugar and 2 tablespoons of water, then making into a purée.

Action

1. Cook the plums as above if you did not do so in the preparation.

2. Heat the oil in a frying-pan and lightly brown the pork fillets.

3. Transfer the pork to a casserole. Add the wine, cloves and seasoning. Pour the plum purée on top of the meat. Cover the casserole and cook in a very moderate oven for 1 hour.

The Day Before

Port and Prunes Pork

2 4-oz. slices of pork fillet	(6)
½ green pepper	(1 large)
6 prunes	(15)
1 oz. butter	(3)
1 cup stock	(3)
2 tablespoons port	(4)
seasoning	
seasoned flour	

120

Preparation

Cut the flesh off the prune stones with scissors. Deseed and thinly slice the green pepper. Make seasoned flour.

Action

1. Roll the pork fillets in the seasoned flour.

2. Heat the butter in a frying-pan and cook the fillets on each side for 2 minutes.

3. Transfer the pork to a casserole and add the prunes and green pepper. Pour over the stock, port and seasoning.

4. Cover the casserole and cook in a low oven for 40 minutes. When cooked, remove from oven, cool, and chill in refrigerator overnight.

Next Day

Reheat casserole in a moderate oven.

The Day Before

Beef Bacon Sandwich

2 thin slices of topside	(6)
3 rashers bacon	(9)
1 cup stock	(2)
1 bay leaf	(2)
1 pinch nutmeg	($\frac{1}{4}$ teaspoon)
1 pinch thyme	($\frac{1}{4}$ teaspoon)
1 pinch rosemary	($\frac{1}{4}$ teaspoon)
seasoning	

Preparation

Cut each slice of beef in half so that each piece measures about 3 in. by 3 in. Dice the bacon and remove the rinds and reserve them.

Action

1. Lay the beef and bacon in a casserole in alternating layers,
   sprinkling pepper, nutmeg and herbs between each layer. (If
   you can make one large sandwich, so much the better, but if
   you have to have two or three it doesn't really matter.)
2. Put the bay leaves and bacon rinds on top of the sandwiches.
3. Pour over the stock. Cover the casserole and cook in a very
   low oven for 1½ hours. When cooked remove the bacon rinds,
   cool, and chill in the refrigerator overnight.

Next Day

Reheat in a moderate oven.

The Hour Before

Belted Beef

4 (2 oz. each approx.) slices of topside	(12)
¼ lb. flat mushrooms	(¾)
½ small green pepper	(1)
2 tomatoes	(6)
1 small clove garlic	(2)
2 tablespoons oil	(6)
seasoning	

Preparation

Peel and slice the tomatoes. Finely chop the garlic. Deseed the
pepper and finely chop. Wash the mushrooms and remove stalks.
Tenderize the beef by banging. (Your butcher will do this for you
if asked.)

Action

1. In a casserole place 2 (6) of the slices of topside and cover
   them with the other ingredients. Season, then lay the other
   slices of topside on the stuffing, making a sandwich.
2. Cover with oil and place in a moderate oven for 1 hour.

The Day Before

Black Ball Beef

¾lb rump steak	(2)
4 anchovy fillets	(12)
4 large black olives	(12)
2 medium onions	(4)
3 tablespoons oil	(6)
1 cup stock	(2½)
2 tablespoons port	(6)
1 dessertspoon chopped parsley	(3)
seasoning	
seasoned flour	

Preparation

Trim the steak and cut into cubes. Make seasoned flour. Stone the olives. Finely chop the anchovies. Peel and slice the onion.

Action

1. Heat the oil in a heavy frying-pan and sauté the onions for 7 minutes. Transfer them to a casserole. Meanwhile, toss the meat in the seasoned flour, coating it generously.

2. Sauté the meat in the remains of the oil for 7–10 minutes, then transfer to the casserole.

3. Add to the casserole the stock, stoned olives, anchovies, port and seasoning. Cook in a low oven for 1 hour. When cooked, remove from oven, cool, and chill overnight in the refrigerator.

Next Day

Reheat the casserole in a moderate oven, and at the point of service garnish with freshly chopped parsley.

The Day Before

Aunt Annie's Chilli

½ lb. best quality minced beef	(1½)
1 onion	(3)
⅓ tin kidney beans	(1)
1 small size tin of tomatoes	(1 medium)
1 tablespoon tomato purée	(3)
1 small tin red peppers	(1 medium)
1 small clove garlic	(3)
⅓ cup meat stock	(1)
1 dessertspoon Bourbon whisky or Madeira	(3)
½ teaspoon chilli powder	(1½)
1 pinch thyme	(½ teaspoon)
1 pinch basil	(½ teaspoon)
1 small pinch paprika	(¼ teaspoon)
1 small pinch cayenne	(¼ teaspoon)
1 bay leaf	(3)
1 dessertspoon oil	(3)
seasoning	

Preparation

Skin and roughly chop onion(s). Skin and finely chop the garlic.
Mix the chilli powder with the stock.

Action

1. Heat the oil in a large heavy saucepan and sauté the onion(s)
   and garlic for 5 minutes. Add the meat and brown it.

2. Add all the other ingredients to the meat and onions. Stir well.
   Cover the pan and simmer over a very low heat for 1 (1¼)
   hour(s), stirring occasionally.

3. Adjust the seasoning, transfer to a casserole, cool, and chill
   in the refrigerator overnight.

Next Day

Remove any excess fat that may have appeared. Reheat in a
moderate oven.

The Day Before

Club Beef

2 good slices of topside	(6)
¼ lb. mushrooms	(¾)
1 onion	(3)
1 tablespoon oil	(3)
1½ oz. butter	(2½)
1 wineglass red wine	(3)
2 tablespoons port	(4)
¾ cup stock	(2)
1 small clove of garlic	(2)
1 tablespoon chopped parsley	(2)
seasoning	
seasoned flour	

Preparation

Wash and slice mushrooms. Peel and slice onion(s) and garlic. Make seasoned flour.

Action

1. Heat the butter and oil in a frying-pan and toss the mushrooms in it for 3 minutes, then remove to a plate.

2. Sauté the onion(s) in the remains of the butter and oil in the frying-pan, until they begin to go clear. Meanwhile toss the topside in the seasoned flour. When the onions are clear, add the meat to the frying-pan and sauté for 2 minutes on each side.

3. Blend in the wine, stock and port, and add the garlic. Bring the liquid to the boil and season.

4. Transfer the contents of the frying-pan to a casserole and arrange the mushrooms on top of the beef.

5. Cook in a low oven for 30 minutes, then remove casserole from oven. Allow to cool, and chill in refrigerator overnight.

Next Day

Reheat the casserole in a low oven. At the point of service, garnish with the chopped parsley.

The Hour Before

Fricadelle

6 oz. fresh minced beef	(¾ lb.)
6 oz. pork sausage meat	(¾ lb.)
4 tablespoons fresh white breadcrumbs	(12)
1 egg	(2)
1 small onion	(2 medium)
1 tablespoon chopped parsley	(3)
⅛ pint milk	(¼)
seasoning	

Preparation

Skin and finely chop the onion. Make the breadcrumbs. Separate egg white(s) and yolk(s). Chop the parsley.

Action

1. In a bowl mix together the minced beef, sausage meat, bread-crumbs, yolk of egg, parsley, onions and seasoning.

2. Stiffly beat the egg white and fold it into the meat.

3. Shape the mixture into a loaf and put it in a roasting-pan, and baste with the milk. Cook in a moderate oven for 25 (40) minutes, basting occasionally with the milk. Remove loaf from roasting-pan on to a hot dish to serve.

Note: This dish should be carved into thin slices, and is also excellent cold with a salad.
Don't worry when the basting milk curdles—it's bound to!

The Day Before
Beef Moussaka

1 large aubergine	(3)
½ lb. best quality minced beef	(1½)
1 onion	(3)
1 small tin tomato purée	(2)
½ cup fresh white breadcrumbs	(1½)
4 tablespoons oil	(8)
1 oz. butter	(2)
1 dessertspoon flour	(2)
1½ cups milk	(3)
2 tablespoons grated strong English cheese	(4)
2 tablespoons grated Parmesan cheese	(4)
1 glass white wine	(2)
1 glass water	(3)
1 pinch cinnamon	(¼ teaspoon)
1 pinch nutmeg	(¼ teaspoon)
1 tablespoon chopped parsley	(3)
seasoning	

Preparation

Peel the aubergine(s) and slice. Cover them with salt and put them in a colander with a weighted plate on top to drain off excess bitterness. Leave them for at least 30 minutes. Peel and slice the onion. Grate the cheeses. Make fresh white breadcrumbs. Chop the parsley.

Action

1. In a saucepan heat 2 (4) tablespoons of the oil and sauté the onions for 7 minutes. Then add the minced beef and cook for a further 10 minutes stirring frequently.

2. Add the tomato purée, the wine, water, cinnamon, nutmeg, parsley and seasoning to the meat and onions. Mix thoroughly, then cover the pan and simmer over a very low heat for 50 minutes, or until most of the liquid is used up. Keep an eye on it and stir occasionally in case the mixture is sticking.

3. When the aubergines have drained, wash off the salt and pat them dry in a cloth. Then heat the rest of the oil in a frying-pan and cook the aubergines until they are lightly browned.

4. While the meat mixture is cooking, make a sauce with the butter, flour and milk. After the sauce has boiled for 2 minutes, withdraw the pan from the heat and stir in half the cheeses and season. Leave on one side.

5. When the meat is ready, butter a heat-proof dish and sprinkle on half the breadcrumbs. Then put in a layer of aubergines, followed by a layer of the meat mixture. Continue until all the aubergine and meat are used up, finishing with an aubergine layer.

6. Sprinkle over the remains of the breadcrumbs and cover the whole thing with the cheese sauce. Sprinkle on the rest of the cheese. Cool, and chill overnight in refrigerator.

Next Day
Bake in a moderate oven for 1 hour.

The Day Before
Oxtail

1 lb. oxtail	(3)
1 medium onion	(3)
1 shallot	(2)
1 carrot	(3)
3 tablespoons oil	(6)
½ wineglass water	(1½)
½ wineglass red wine	(1½)
1 bay leaf	(1)
1 pinch thyme	(1)
seasoning	
seasoned flour	

Preparation
Make the seasoned flour, adding to it the pinch of thyme. Peel

and slice the onion(s), shallot(s) and carrot(s). Trim the oxtail, and cut into the natural sections if the butcher has not already done this for you.

Action

1. Heat the oil in a frying-pan and sauté the onion(s), shallot(s) and carrot(s) for 5 minutes.

2. Meanwhile toss the oxtail in the seasoned flour, then add it to the frying-pan. Brown the meat all round and then transfer the contents of the frying-pan to a casserole.

3. Add to the casserole the water, wine, bay leaf and seasoning. Cover the dish and cook in a very low oven for 3 hours.

4. After 3 hours remove from the oven and extract the bay leaf. Allow the dish to cool before chilling overnight in refrigerator.

Next Day

If a layer of fat has formed on top of the oxtail remove it before reheating in a very low oven.

The Day Before
His Cottage Pie

10 oz. underdone cold roast beef	(1½ lb.)
2 medium onions	(6)
½ medium green pepper	(1 large)
1 carrot	(2)
1 tablespoon currants or sultanas	(2)
1 dessertspoon oil	(3)
1½ oz. butter	(3)
1 dessertspoon flour	(3)
½ cup milk	(1½)
1 bay leaf	(1)
1 sprig thyme	(1)
seasoning	
about 4 medium-sized potatoes for top	(10)

Preparation

Peel the potatoes. Trim the meat and mince it. Peel and slice the onions and carrot(s). Wash, deseed and slice the green pepper. Wash the currants.

Action

1. Boil the potatoes, and when cooked mash them in the usual way with plenty of butter and seasoning.

2. In a frying-pan melt the butter and oil and fry the onions until soft.

3. When the onions are soft, blend in the flour and milk and bring the mixture gently to the boil, stirring constantly.

4. To the mixture add the minced beef, finely chopped carrot, green pepper, sultanas or currants and seasoning.

5. In the bottom of a pie-dish place the bay leaf and thyme, and pour over the mixture from the frying-pan. Allow to cool.

6. When the meat is cold cover with a layer of mashed potato. Dot with butter, and chill in the refrigerator overnight.

Next Day

Reheat in a moderate oven for 40 minutes, if necessary finishing off the browning of the potato under the grill.

The Day Before

Her Cottage Pie

½ lb. best quality fresh minced beef	(1½)
2 tomatoes	(5)
2 oz. mushrooms	(6)
⅓ small green pepper	(1)
1 small onion	(3)
1½ oz. butter	(2½)
1 dessertspoon flour	(2)
½ cup meat stock	(1)
2 tablespoons port	(5)
1 small clove garlic	(1 large)
½ teaspoon (approx.) Worcester sauce	(1½)
1 bay leaf	(1)
1 pinch thyme	(1)
1 heaped tablespoon grated mild English cheese	(3)
seasoning	
about 4 medium-sized potatoes for top	(10)

Preparation

Peel the potatoes. Peel and chop the onions and tomatoes. Wash and slice the mushrooms. Wash and deseed the pepper, then chop very finely. Peel and finely chop the garlic. Grate the cheese.

Action

1. Boil the potatoes, and when cooked mash in the usual way with plenty of butter and seasoning.

2. In a frying-pan sauté the mushrooms in the butter, then transfer them to a pie-dish. In the remains of the butter fry the onions and green pepper for 7 minutes, then add the minced beef, peeled tomatoes, garlic and seasoning. Cook over a low heat, stirring frequently, for 10 minutes.

3. Sprinkle with the flour. Pour in the stock, port and Worcester sauce. Blend well, add the bay leaf, thyme and seasoning, and continue cooking for 15 minutes.

4. Transfer the contents of the frying-pan to the pie-dish with the mushrooms and mix together. Allow to cool and when cold, cover with a layer of mashed potato. Sprinkle on the grated cheese and dot with butter. Chill overnight in the refrigerator.

Next Day

Reheat in a hot oven for 30 minutes, if necessary finishing off the browning of the potato under the grill.

The Day Before

Her Stew

½ lb. stewing-steak	(1½)
2 carrots	(6)
2 medium onions	(6)
1 stick celery	(3)
¼ green pepper	(1 small)
2 oz. mushrooms	(4)
2 oz. dripping	(4)
1 cup good meat stock	(2½)
1 clove garlic	(2)
1 bay leaf	(2)
seasoning	
seasoned flour	

Preparation

Trim and dice the meat. Make the seasoned flour. Peel and dice carrots, onions, cloves of garlic and celery. Wash and slice the mushrooms. Deseed and slice green pepper.

Action

1. Heat the dripping in a frying-pan and sauté all the vegetables for 10 minutes. Meanwhile coat the meat well in the seasoned flour.

2. Add the meat to the frying-pan and brown it.

3. Blend in the stock and bring it to the boil, stirring constantly.

4. Transfer the contents of the frying-pan to a casserole. Add the bay leaf and seasoning. Cover and cook in a very low oven for 2½ hours.

5. Remove the dish from the oven. Allow to cool, and chill overnight in the refrigerator.

Next Day

Remove any excess fat. Adjust the seasoning and reheat in a low oven.

The Day Before

His Stew

½ lb. best stewing-steak	(1½)
1 large onion	(3)
1 carrot	(2)
2 tablespoons oil	(5)
½ wineglass red wine	(1½)
⅓ pint meat stock	(1)
1 bay leaf	(1)
1 pinch basil, marjoram and thyme	(1)
seasoning	
seasoned flour	

Preparation

Make the seasoned flour to which should be added the basil, marjoram and thyme. Peel and slice the onion and carrot. Trim the meat and cut into pieces.

Action

1. Heat the oil in a frying-pan and fry the onions until they are

light brown. Transfer them to a heavy saucepan and pour over the stock.

2. Toss the meat in the seasoned flour and add to the fat in the frying-pan. Lightly brown the meat then transfer it to the saucepan with the onions.

3. Blend the wine in with the remains of the oil and flour which will be left in the frying-pan, bring to the boil, then pour into the saucepan. Add the carrot(s) and bay leaf, then season.

4. Cover the saucepan and simmer for 1½ hours. Turn into a casserole, allow to cool, and chill overnight in the refrigerator.

Next Day

Reheat in a moderate oven.

The Day Before

Casseroled Chops with Mushrooms

4 best end of neck of lamb chops	(12)
¼ lb. button mushrooms	(¾)
2 tablespoons redcurrant jelly	(4)
1 tablespoon Worcester sauce	(2)
1 tablespoon lemon juice	(3)
1½ oz. butter	(2½)
1 dessertspoon flour	(2)
¼ pint meat stock	(½)
1 pinch nutmeg	(¼ teaspoon)
seasoning	

Preparation

Trim any excess fat from the lamb chops. Wash the mushrooms. Squeeze the lemon.

Action

1. Heat the butter in a frying-pan and brown the chops quickly

in it. Transfer them to a casserole and put the mushrooms on top.

2. In a saucepan, slowly melt the redcurrant jelly with the Worcester sauce and lemon juice. Add the nutmeg and seasoning.

3. Add the flour to the fat in the frying-pan and blend in the stock and mixture from the saucepan. Bring to the boil and cook for 2 minutes. Adjust seasoning and pour over the cutlets.

4. Cook in a low oven for 1¼ hours. When cooked, cool, and chill in the refrigerator overnight.

Next Day

Reheat in a moderate oven.

The Hour Before

Marrow Lamb

½ small leg of lamb	(1 leg)
½ small marrow	(1 medium)
6 small new potatoes	(18)
1 large tomato	(3)
1 small clove of garlic	(1 large)
4 tablespoons oil	(8)
seasoning	

Preparation

Peel and take seeds from the marrow and cut into pieces. Peel tomatoes and slice. Peel new potatoes. Poke the garlic into the lamb near the bone.

Action

1. Spread a large sheet of foil in a roasting-tin, leaving enough

spare foil all round to make a parcel of the ingredients. On to the foil put the potatoes, tomatoes, marrow and seasoning. Then put the leg of lamb on top of this.

2. Pour the oil over the lamb and bring the foil up to make a parcel, turning over the edges to seal it.

3. Bake in a hot oven allowing 20 minutes per pound, plus 20 minutes over.

4. Serve on a dish surrounded by the vegetables, and as you will have quite a lot of juice, it is better to put this in a separate dish.

The Day Before
Moussaka

1 large aubergine	(3)
½ lb. cooked lamb	(1½)
1 large onion	(3)
3 tomatoes	(8)
1 dessertspoon sultanas	(3)
3 tablespoons oil	(8)
1 oz. butter	(2)
1 dessertspoon flour	(2)
1½ cups milk	(3)
4 tablespoons grated Cheddar cheese	(8)
seasoning	

Preparation

Peel the aubergine(s) and slice. Cover them with salt and put in a colander with a weighted plate on top to drain off the excess bitterness, for at least 30 minutes. Mince the lamb. Skin and slice the onion(s) and tomatoes. Grate the cheese.

Action

1. Make a white sauce with the butter, flour and milk. When the

sauce has boiled for 2 minutes, withdraw the saucepan from
the heat and stir in three-quarters of the cheese. Season.

2. When the aubergines have drained, wash off the excess salt
   and pat the vegetables dry. Then heat the oil in a frying-pan
   and sauté the onions for 5 minutes before adding the aubergines. Continue cooking for 10 minutes, then add the tomatoes,
   sultanas and minced lamb. Cook for another 10 minutes,
   stirring occasionally.

3. When the meat is ready, butter a fireproof dish then put in a
   layer of aubergines followed by a layer of the meat mixture.
   Continue until all the aubergines and meat are used up,
   finishing with an aubergine layer.

4. Cover with the cheese sauce, and sprinkle over the rest of the
   cheese. Allow to cool, and chill in refrigerator overnight.

Next Day

Reheat in a moderate oven for 40 minutes.

The Day Before

Pooh Chops

4 small loin lamb chops	(12)
¼ lb. mushrooms	(¾)
4 medium-size tomatoes	(12)
1 dessertspoon honey	(2)
1 wineglass white wine	(2½)
1 small clove of garlic	(2)
seasoning	

Preparation

Peel and finely chop garlic. Wash and coarsely chop mushrooms.
Peel and slice tomatoes.

Action

1. Place the chops on their backs in a frying-pan and cook until
   the fat appears from them. Then add the chopped garlic and
   continue cooking until the fat on the chops is crisp and brown.
   Now turn them on their sides and brown each side for two
   minutes.

2. Strain off the liquid fat and transfer the chops and the remains
   of the garlic to a casserole and add the honey, mushrooms and
   tomatoes. Pour the wine over and season.

3. Cook for 40 minutes in a low oven. Remove and cool before
   putting in the refrigerator overnight.

Next Day

Reheat the casserole in a low oven.

The Day Before

Lamb in Onion Sauce

½ lb. lamb cut from a leg	(2½ lb. leg)
2 medium onions	(4)
1 dessertspoon oil	(3)
2 cloves	(4)
1 dessertspoon flour	(3)
⅓ pint milk	(1)
2 oz. butter	(4)
seasoning	

Preparation

Fillet the lamb from the bone and trim all fat from it, then cut
into 1 in. cubes. Peel and coarsely chop onions.

Action

1. Put the lamb in a saucepan, cover with warm water and bring

to the boil. When it has boiled for five minutes, skim the scum off the water, tip the meat into a colander and wash quickly under boiling water. Drain and pat dry.

2. Heat the oil in a frying-pan and sauté the lamb, but do not allow to brown. This takes 5–10 minutes. Transfer the meat to a casserole.

3. Make a white sauce with the butter, flour and milk. When it has boiled for 2 minutes, stir in the onions and seasoning. Pour over the meat in the casserole and add the cloves.

4. Cover and cook in a very moderate oven for 1½ hours. When cooked allow to cool, and chill overnight in the refrigerator.

Next Day

Reheat in a moderate oven.

The Day Before

Spiced Chops

2 chump lamb chops	(6)
1 small onion	(3)
2 oz. mushrooms	(6)
1 teaspoon flour	(1 dessertspoon)
1 tablespoon oil	(3)
2 tablespoons sherry	(6)
⅓ cup meat stock	(1)
2 tablespoons commercially soured cream	(¼ pint)
½ teaspoon sugar	(1)
1 teaspoon Worcester sauce	(3)
1 teaspoon paprika	(3)
½ small clove garlic	(1)
seasoning	

Preparation

Peel and slice onion(s.) Wash and slice mushrooms. Peel and finely chop garlic.

Action

1. In a large frying-pan heat the oil and sauté the mushrooms, onion(s) and garlic. At the same time grill the chops for 3 minutes on either side, and then turn them upwards to crisp the fat. When the chops are cooked transfer them to a casserole.

2. Sprinkle the flour over the vegetables in the frying-pan, then blend in the stock, sherry, sugar, Worcester sauce, paprika and seasoning. Bring to the boil and cook for 2 minutes, stirring constantly.

3. Pour the contents of the frying-pan over the chops. Cook in a moderate oven for 35 minutes. When cooked cool, and chill overnight in the refrigerator.

Next Day

Reheat in a moderate oven and at the point of service stir in the sour cream.

The Hour Before

Sweet and Sour Lamb

1 top half of small leg of lamb	(1 leg approx. 3 lb.)
(1 lb. approx.)	
1 onion	(2)
1 carrot	(2)
1 stick celery	(2)
1 wineglass red wine	(2)
1 dessertspoon redcurrant jelly	(3)
2 tablespoons commercially soured cream	(¼ pint)
1 bay leaf	(2)
1 sprig thyme	(1)
seasoning	

Preparation

Peel and dice the vegetables.

Action

1. Put the diced vegetables in the bottom of a casserole, and place the meat, seasoning, bay leaf and thyme on top and pour over the wine.

2. Cover tightly and cook in a moderate oven, allowing 20 minutes per pound.

3. When the meat is cooked, put it on a serving-dish in the oven to keep warm and strain the juice into a saucepan. Bring to the boil and simmer for 5 minutes, then remove from the heat and stir in the red currant jelly and the sour cream. Serve the sauce with the meat in a separate dish.

Note: If you want to eat the vegetables as an accompaniment to this dish, we recommend you use rather more of them, otherwise they can be saved for soup.

Note on the Cuts of Veal referred to in the following Recipes

Veal is becoming much more easily obtainable, particularly in London, than it has been in recent years. Even so, many butchers charge quite unrealistic prices for fillet, and are not above selling pie veal composed mainly of skin and fat.

Unless your butcher is helpful and prepared to cut your meat to your own specification, it is much more economical to buy a small joint. Fillets can be cut from the top of a leg—for the best results cut the meat 'on the cross', at an angle of 45 degrees to the bone—and pie veal can be cut from a small half shoulder. Unless you are very skilled with a knife, it is probably easier to use a pair of serrated scissors for cutting the pie veal.

The Day Before

Artichoke Veal

2 large thin slices of fillet of veal	(6)
2 Jerusalem artichokes	(6)
½ small tin of mixed green and red peppers, tomatoes and aubergines	(1)
2 oz. butter	(4)
1 tablespoon flour	(2)
½ pint milk	(1)
1½ oz. grated mild English cheese	(3)
2 tablespoons sherry	(5)
seasoning	

Preparation

Peel and slice the artichokes. Grate the cheese.

Action

1. Boil the artichokes in salted water until tender (15 minutes approx.).

2. Make a sauce with half the butter, the flour and the milk. When the sauce has boiled for 2 minutes, withdraw the pan from the heat, stir in the cheese, sherry and seasoning. Cover the pan and leave on one side.

3. Heat the rest of the butter in a frying-pan and sauté the veal for 1 minute on each side. Take out of the pan and put on to a plate.

4. When the artichokes are cooked, mash them finely and mix with the tin of peppers, tomatoes and aubergines.

5. Spread the mixture generously over the veal fillets and roll them up, securing with two cocktail sticks.

6. Put the stuffed veal rolls in a casserole, arranging them so that the ends of the cocktail sticks are poking up. Cover them with the cheese sauce. Allow to cool and chill overnight in the refrigerator.

Next Day

Cover the dish and reheat in a low oven. At the point of service, pull out the cocktail sticks.

Note: If you have difficulty in finding the tin of mixed vegetables, use a small quantity of fresh ones and sauté them all together in a closed pan with some oil until soft.

The Day Before

Veal Fricassee

¾ lb. stewing veal (see p. 141)	(1¾)
¼ lb. mushrooms	(¾)
1 onion	(3)
2 oz. butter	(4)
¾ cup chicken stock	(2)
½ wineglass white wine	(1)
3 tablespoons commercially soured cream	(¼ pint)
1 pinch mixed herbs	(½ teaspoon)
1 pinch garlic powder	(¼ teaspoon)
seasoning	

Preparation

Trim the veal and cut it into cubes. Peel and chop the onion. Wash and slice mushrooms.

Action

1. In a frying-pan heat the butter and sauté the veal, onion and mushrooms for 10 minutes, stirring occasionally.

2. Add the stock, wine, garlic powder, herbs and seasoning.

3. Transfer the contents of the frying-pan to a casserole. Cover and cook in a low oven for 1¼ hours. When cooked allow to cool, then chill overnight in refrigerator.

Next Day

Reheat the casserole in a low oven, and at the point of service stir in the sour cream.

The Day Before

Glass House Veal

½ lb. fillet veal	(1½)
½ small cucumber	(1 small)
1 fresh pear	(2 large)
2 oz. mushrooms	(6)
½ green pepper	(1)
3 tomatoes	(8)
½ cup uncooked long-grain rice	(1½)
2 tablespoons oil	(6)
½ cup chicken stock	(1½)
1 pinch basil	(½ teaspoon)
seasoning	
2 oz. butter	(4)

Preparation

Trim the veal and cut into cubes. Peel and dice cucumber and pear. Wash and slice mushrooms. Wash, deseed and slice green pepper. Skin and chop tomatoes. Wash the rice.

Action

1. Heat 1 (2) oz. of the butter in a heavy frying-pan and sauté the veal until lightly browned.

2. Add 1 (3) tablespoons of the oil to the meat in the frying-pan and the diced cucumber, pear, green pepper, mushrooms, tomatoes and basil. Cover the pan with a lid and cook over a very low heat for 10 minutes.

3. While the other ingredients are cooking, melt the rest of the butter and oil in a very heavy saucepan and fry the rice, stirring frequently, until brown.

4. Transfer the contents of the frying-pan to the saucepan with
   the rice. Season, and add the stock if necessary, but the
   vegetables should have made enough juice in which to cook
   the rice. Cover the pan and cook very slowly until the rice is
   soft (about 25 minutes). Stir occasionally and add more stock
   if necessary.

5. When the rice is cooked, transfer the contents of the pan to a
   casserole. Allow to cool, and chill overnight in the refrigerator.

Next Day

Reheat in a very low oven.

The Day Before

Ratatat Veal

½ lb. fillet veal	(1½)
1 aubergine	(2)
½ small green pepper	(1 large)
3 large tomatoes	(8)
2 tablespoons oil	(4)
1 oz. butter	(2)
2 small cloves garlic	(4)
1 wineglass red wine	(2½)
1 pinch basil	(½ teaspoon)
seasoning	
seasoned flour	

Preparation

Slice the aubergine(s) and put in a colander sprinkled with salt,
with a weighted plate on top for 30 minutes to remove excess
bitterness. Cut the veal into cubes. Wash, deseed and slice green
pepper. Peel and slice tomatoes. Peel and finely chop the garlic.
Make seasoned flour.

Action

1. Roll the veal in the seasoned flour.
2. Heat half the oil and butter in a heavy frying-pan and sauté the veal, together with the finely chopped garlic, until browned.
3. At the same time heat the rest of the oil and butter in a saucepan and put in the aubergine (which you should first rinse and pat dry in a clean cloth), and the green pepper. Cover the pan and cook over a very low heat for 15 minutes, stirring occasionally.
4. When the veal is lightly browned, blend in the wine, and after the contents of the saucepan have cooked for 15 minutes, tip in the contents of the frying-pan. Add to this the tomatoes, basil and seasoning. Cover the pan again and cook over a very low heat for 40 minutes. When cooked, transfer the contents of the saucepan to a casserole. Cool, and chill overnight in the refrigerator.

Next Day

Reheat the dish in a moderate oven.

The Day Before

Stacked Veal

2 thin veal fillets	(6)
1 carrot	(2)
1 large onion	(2)
2 medium onions	(6)
¼ lb. mushrooms	(¾)
2 tablespoons oil	(4)
2 oz. butter	(4)
1 tablespoon flour	(2)
½ pint milk	(⅔)
2 tablespoons white wine	(5)
3 tablespoons sherry	(6)
1 bay leaf	(2)
seasoning	

Preparation

Peel onions and slice, keeping the two sizes separate. Scrape carrot(s) and dice. Wash, peel and slice mushrooms.

Action

1. Heat 1 (2) tablespoons of the oil in a saucepan and put in the 1 (2) large onion(s) and sliced carrot. Put a lid on the pan and sauté the vegetables over a very low heat for 15 minutes, stirring occasionally.

2. In another saucepan heat another 1 (2) tablespoons of oil and put in the medium-sized onions and the mushrooms, and a little seasoning. Put a lid on the pan and sauté the vegetables over a very low heat for 15 minutes, stirring occasionally.

3. In yet another saucepan make a white sauce with 1 (2) oz. of the butter, the flour and milk. When the sauce has simmered for 4 minutes, withdraw the pan from the heat, stir in the sherry and season. Cover the pan and leave on one side.

4. Heat the remainder of the butter in a frying-pan and sauté the veal fillets for 2 minutes on each side. Remove from the pan to a plate.

5. When the carrots and onions have cooked for 15 minutes, take them from the saucepan and arrange them as a bed in a casserole, laying the bay leaf in the middle.

6. When the mushrooms and onions are soft, either purée them by pushing them through a sieve, which is a very long job, then stir in the wine, or, preferably, put them in a liquidizer with the wine and blend to a smooth paste.

7. Lay 1 (3) of the veal fillets on the bed of vegetables, then spread a generous amount of the purée on top of each one, and make a sandwich with the other piece(s) of veal.

8. Cover with the sherry sauce. Allow to cool, and chill overnight in the refrigerator.

Next Day

Reheat in a moderate oven. To serve cut each sandwich in half.

The Day Before

Spears Veal

¾ lb. stewing veal (see p. 141)   (1¾)
2 oz. mushrooms   (6)
1 onion   (3)
2 tablespoons oil   (4)
1 oz. butter   (2)
1½ cups chicken stock   (3)
½ small tin of asparagus soup   (1)
1 pinch basil   (1)
seasoning

Preparation

Trim meat and cut into cubes. Peel and slice onion. Wash and slice mushrooms.

Action

1. Heat the butter and oil in a frying-pan and sauté the onions, veal and mushrooms for 10 minutes, stirring frequently.

2. Transfer the contents of the frying-pan to a casserole. Add the stock, basil and seasoning. Cover and cook in a low oven for 45 minutes.

3. Remove the casserole from the oven and blend in the asparagus soup. Allow to cool, and chill in the refrigerator overnight.

Next Day

Reheat casserole in a low oven.

The Day Before

Square Cut Veal

¾ lb. good pie veal (see p. 141)	(2)
¼ lb. mushrooms	(½)
⅓ green pepper	(1)
4 tomatoes	(12)
1 onion	(3)
2 tablespoons oil	(4)
1 oz. butter	(3)
1 pinch basil	(¼ teaspoon)
1 pinch thyme	(1)
seasoning	
seasoned flour	

Preparation

Trim the veal and cut into cubes. Skin the onions and tomatoes and slice. Wash and slice mushrooms. Make the seasoned flour, adding to it the pinch (¼ teaspoon) of thyme. Wash, deseed and slice green pepper.

Action

1. Roll the meat in the seasoned flour.

2. Heat half the oil and butter in a frying-pan and sauté the veal for 7 minutes, or until lightly browned. At the same time heat the other half of the oil and butter in a saucepan and put in the sliced onion and green pepper. Cover the pan and cook over a low heat for 10 minutes, stirring occasionally.

3. When the onions and peppers have cooked for 10 minutes, add the mushrooms and tomatoes and cook for another 5 minutes.

4. Add the veal to the ingredients in the saucepan. Sprinkle on the basil and seasoning and mix thoroughly for 5 minutes over a low heat.

5. Transfer the contents of the saucepan to a casserole. Cover and

cook in a low oven for 1 hour. When cooked, allow to cool, and chill overnight in the refrigerator.

Next Day

Reheat the casserole in a low oven.

The Day Before

Veal and Sweetbreads Fricassee

6 oz. veal sweetbreads	(1 lb.)
6 oz. pie veal (see p. 141)	(1 lb.)
3 onions	(6)
2 sticks celery	(6)
1 oz. butter	(3)
1 dessertspoon flour	(3)
1 pint mild chicken stock	(2)
2 tablespoons sherry	(5)
1 small carrot	(1 large)
1 wedge of lemon with peel	(1)
1 bay leaf	(2)
1 sprig thyme	(1)
seasoning	

Preparation

Peel the onions and slice all but 1 (1) of them. Scrub the carrot. Scrape and slice the celery into half-inch pieces. Cut a wedge of lemon. Trim the veal and sweetbreads and cut the veal into cubes. In a piece of muslin or old stocking tie together the unsliced onion, the carrot, bay leaf, lemon and thyme.

Action

1. Put the veal and sweetbreads in a heavy saucepan with the unsliced onion, etc., the celery and the stock. Cover the pan and simmer gently for 1¼ hours.

2. When the meat is cooked, strain the stock into a jug and discard the onion, etc. but not the celery. Transfer the meat and celery to a casserole.

3. Heat the butter in a saucepan and sauté the chopped onions until soft but not brown. Sprinkle on the flour and blend in $\frac{1}{2}$ (1$\frac{1}{4}$) pints of the stock. Bring to the boil stirring constantly and cook for 2 minutes, then withdraw the pan from the heat and stir in the sherry and adjust seasoning.

4. Pour the sauce over the meat. Cool, and store overnight in the refrigerator.

Next Day

Cover the dish and reheat in a low oven, and at the point of service freshly-ground black pepper should be generously sprinkled over the dish.

The Day Before

Winter Garden Veal

$\frac{3}{4}$ lb. breast of veal	(1$\frac{3}{4}$)
2 oz. mushrooms	(6)
3 sticks celery	(6)
1 small onion	(2)
1 small carrot	(2)
1 small wedge of lemon with peel	(2)
$\frac{3}{4}$ oz. butter	(1$\frac{1}{2}$)
1 level dessertspoon cornflour	(2)
1 bay leaf	(1)
2 tablespoons single cream	($\frac{1}{4}$ pint)
seasoning	

Preparation

Wash and slice the mushrooms. Skin the onion and carrot and cut in half. Trim the meat. Cut the lemon wedge(s). Skin the celery and cut into 4-inch pieces.

151

Action

1. Put the veal, onion, carrot, lemon, celery, bay leaf and seasoning in a saucepan with sufficient water to cover. Cover the pan
   and simmer over a very low heat for 1 (1½) hours.

2. While the veal is cooking, sauté the mushrooms in the butter
   and leave on one side.

3. When the veal is cooked, strain the liquid into a jug. Extract
   the celery and put it in a casserole. Discard all the other
   vegetables, or retain them for making soup.

4. Measure out ⅓ (1) pint of the liquid in which the veal was
   cooked. Blend it into the cornflour and tip it into a saucepan
   and boil for 2 minutes to thicken.

5. Cut the veal into pieces and add this and the mushrooms to
   the thickened stock. Mix thoroughly and adjust the seasoning,
   then pour the contents of the pan into the casserole with the
   celery. Allow to cool, and chill in refrigerator overnight.

Next Day

Reheat the casserole in a low oven, and at the point of service,
stir in the cream.

The Day Before

Veal with Shrimps

2 fillets of veal (4 oz. each approx.)	(6)
2 oz. peeled cooked shrimps	(6)
4 Jerusalem artichokes	(12)
1¾ oz. butter	(4½)
1 dessertspoon flour	(3)
¼ pint milk	(¾)
½ wineglass white wine	(1½)
2 tablespoons grated mild English cheese	(6)
seasoning	

Preparation

Peel the artichokes. Grate the cheese.

Action

1. Boil the artichokes in salted water until tender. (About 20 minutes.)

2. Make a white sauce with ¾ oz. (2 oz.) of the butter, the flour and the milk. When the sauce has boiled for 2 minutes, withdraw the pan from the heat, stir in the wine, cheese and seasoning. Cover the pan and leave on one side.

3. Heat the rest of the butter in a frying-pan and sauté the veal for 3 minutes on each side. Transfer to a casserole and arrange the shrimps on top of the veal fillets.

4. When the artichokes are soft, slice them and put them with the shrimps on top of the veal. Then cover the whole with the cheese sauce. Allow to cool, and chill overnight in the refrigerator.

Next Day

Reheat in a very moderate oven for 30 minutes.

The Hour Before

Veronica Veal

2 thin fillets of veal (4 oz. each approx.)   (6)
12 white grapes   (36)
2 oz. butter   (4)
½ wineglass white wine   (1½)
3 tablespoons single cream   (½ pint)
2 tablespoons grated mild English cheese   (5)
seasoning
seasoned flour

153

Preparation

Skin and pip the grapes. Grate the cheese. Make the seasoned flour.

Action

1. Roll the veal fillets in the seasoned flour.

2. Heat the butter in a frying-pan and cook the veal fillets in it for 3 minutes on each side. Remove the pan from the heat and stir in the wine, grapes, cream and seasoning.

3. Transfer to a heatproof dish and sprinkle on the grated cheese. Cook in a very low oven for 20 minutes, and if you have time when you are out in the kitchen dishing up, brown the top under the grill. This is not essential, but well worth the extra trouble.

The Hour Before

Liver in Wine

½ lb. calves' liver	(1½)
2 shallots	(6)
2 tablespoons oil	(6)
1 wineglass white wine	(2½)
½ teaspoon basil	(1)
1 small clove garlic	(1 large)
2 tablespoons milk (approx.)	(¼ cup)
seasoning	
seasoned flour	

Preparation

If the butcher did not slice the liver for you, do so now. Peel and finely slice the shallots and garlic. Prepare the seasoned flour.

Action

1. First dip the slices of liver in the milk and then roll them in the seasoned flour.

2. Heat the oil in a heavy frying-pan and brown the slices of liver very slowly, then remove from the pan and keep on one side.

3. To the remainder of the oil in the frying-pan add the shallots, garlic and basil. Cook for seven minutes or until lightly browned.

4. Return the liver to the pan and stir in the wine and seasoning.

5. Transfer the contents of the frying-pan to a casserole and cook in a low oven for 30 minutes.

The Day Before
Kidney and Bacon Pie

4 lambs' kidneys	(12)
2 rashers back bacon	(6)
2 tomatoes	(4)
2 oz. mushrooms	(6)
1 onion	(2)
1 oz. butter	(2½)
1 wineglass red wine	(2½)
1 tablespoon port	(3)
1 pinch basil	(¼ teaspoon)
1 pinch marjoram	(¼ teaspoon)
seasoning	
4 oz. flaky pastry with which to cover	(8)

Preparation

Make the pastry (Appendix I) and leave to chill in the refrigerator. Split the kidneys and trim, taking care to cut out the white core and remove the thin outer skin. (This is most easily done with a pair of sharp scissors). Cut off bacon rinds and dice the meat. Skin the tomatoes and onion(s) and chop. Wash and slice the mushrooms.

155

Action

1. Lightly fry the bacon in its own fat in a heavy frying-pan. Remove from pan. Add the butter to the resulting fat and sauté the kidneys, onion and mushrooms for 10 minutes over a low heat.

2. Return the bacon to the pan. Add the wine, port, herbs and seasoning. Bring to the boil, then simmer gently for 10 minutes.

3. Transfer the contents of the frying-pan to a pie-dish and leave to cool. Add the tomatoes.

4. When the kidneys are quite cold, roll out the pastry to the appropriate size and cover the pie-dish. Chill overnight in the refrigerator.

Next Day

Bake in a hot oven for 30 minutes, or until the pastry is properly cooked.

The Day Before

Devil's Delight

6 lambs' kidneys	(18)
4 dried prunes	(12)
2 oz. butter	(4)
½ cup meat stock	(2)
2 dessertspoons apricot brandy (miniature bottle)	
seasoning	
seasoned flour	

Preparation

Make seasoned flour. Trim the kidneys, being careful to remove the white core and the thin outer skin, then cut them into pieces. Cut the flesh off the prunes with scissors. (There is no need to pre-soak the prunes for this dish.)

Action

1. Roll the kidneys in seasoned flour.

2. Heat three-quarters of the butter in a frying-pan and sauté the kidneys for 7 minutes. Pour the apricot brandy over them and flame.

3. Blend in the stock and bring gently to the boil, then simmer for 10 minutes.

4. Heat the rest of the butter in another frying-pan whilst the kidneys are simmering and toss the prunes in the butter until they are just tender. (5–10 minutes.)

5. Transfer the contents of both pans to a casserole and season. Allow to cool, and chill in the refrigerator overnight.

Next Day

Reheat in a moderate oven for 30 minutes.

Note: This dish is rather sweet and is best served with rice and a salad.

The Day Before

Dizzy Kidneys

6 lambs' kidneys	(18)
1 medium onion	(3)
¼ lb. mushrooms	(¾)
2 tablespoons oil	(6)
2½ oz. butter	(4½)
1 tablespoon flour	(2½)
⅓ bottle dry champagne cider	(1)
2 tablespoons port	(6)
1 small clove garlic	(2)
1 bay leaf	(1)
1 sprig thyme	(1)
1 sprig parsley	(2)
seasoning	

157

Preparation

Trim the kidneys, being careful to remove the white core and the thin outer skin, then cut them into pieces. Peel and chop the onion and garlic. Wash the mushrooms and slice. Mix together two-thirds of the butter and all the flour into a paste. Tie together the bay leaf, thyme and parsley.

Action

1. Heat the oil in a large heavy frying-pan and sauté the kidneys for 7 minutes. Add the chopped onions and garlic and sauté for a further 7 minutes, stirring frequently.

2. Drain off any surplus fat and add the champagne cider, the port, herbs and seasoning. Bring gently to the boil, then transfer to a casserole.

3. Cook the casserole in a moderate oven for 30 minutes. Meanwhile sauté the mushrooms in the rest of the butter.

4. When the meat is cooked, stir in the butter and flour mixture and return to the oven for 5 minutes to thicken. Add the mushrooms. Allow to cool, and chill overnight in the refrigerator.

Next Day

Remove the herbs and reheat in a moderate oven.

Note: This dish should really be made with champagne, so it is important to use the champagne cider, rather than the ordinary kind.

The Hour Before

Stuffed Marrow

    1 small vegetable marrow   (1 sufficient for 6)
    ¼ lb. kidneys   (¾)
    3 oz. cooked ham or bacon joint   (8)
    2 tomatoes   (6)
    1 tablespoon oil   (3)
    1½ oz. butter   (3)
    1 tablespoon flour   (2)
    ⅓ pint milk   (⅔)
    2 oz. mild English cheese   (4)
    seasoning

Preparation

Peel the marrow, cut off the top and scoop out the seeds. In the case of the large marrow, you will probably have to cut it in half to get all the seeds out. Trim the kidneys, taking care to remove the white core and the thin outer skin. Grate the cheese. Skin and chop the tomatoes.

Action

1. Place the marrow in a pan of boiling salt water and simmer for 10 minutes. Meanwhile sauté the kidneys in the oil until lightly browned.

2. Drain the marrow and put it on a large sheet of silver foil in a baking tray.

3. Finely mince the kidneys and ham, then mix them with the tomatoes and a little seasoning. Stuff this mixture into the marrow and replace the end you cut off. Wrap the whole thing in the foil and bake in a moderate oven for 1 hour.

4. While the marrow is cooking, make a sauce with the butter, flour, and the milk. When it has boiled for 4 minutes withdraw the pan from the heat and stir in the cheese and seasoning. Leave it like this with a lid on the pan until you are ready

and when you come out to the kitchen to serve up, reheat the sauce and pour it over the marrow.

The Day Before

Tongue and Mushroom Crumble

2 medium-sized uncooked calves'	
tongues	(6, or 1 small ox tongue)
2 oz. mushrooms	(6)
½ cup fresh white breadcrumbs	(1¼)
2 small onions	(2 large)
1 carrot	(2)
2 oz. butter	(4)
1 dessertspoon flour	(3)
½ wineglass white wine	(1½)
1 bay leaf	(1)
seasoning	

Preparation

Soak the tongue for an hour or two if possible, to get rid of the excess salt. Peel and chop the carrot and one onion roughly, and the other onion finely. Wash and slice the mushrooms and make the breadcrumbs. Put the mushrooms and breadcrumbs in separate airtight containers in the refrigerator for the next day.

Action

1. Place the tongues in a saucepan with the roughly cut onion. the carrot, bay leaf, black pepper and sufficient water to cover. Simmer gently for 1½ hours, or 2½ hours if using the ox tongue,

2. When the tongue is cooked strain the stock into a jug and leave the tongue to cool. Meanwhile melt three-quarters of the butter in a saucepan and simmer the other onion until soft. Add the flour and cook for 2 minutes, stirring constantly. Then blend in ¾ (1½) cups of the stock, and the wine. Bring to the boil, stirring constantly, then simmer for 5 minutes.

3. When the tongue is cool enough to handle, remove the skin, bone and gristle, then carve it into slices.

4. Put the slices of tongue in a heatproof dish and pour the sauce over them. Allow to cool, and chill in the refrigerator overnight.

Next Day

Poach the mushrooms for 2 minutes in boiling water. Strain them and put them on top of the tongue. Cover the whole with the breadcrumbs and dot with the remaining butter. Cook in a hot oven for 15 minutes.

The Day Before

Veal Kidney Vol-au-Vents

6 oz. veal kidneys	(1¼ lb.)
1 small onion	(2)
2 tablespoons oil	(4)
1½ oz. butter	(3)
1 level dessertspoon cornflour	(3)
½ cup milk	(1½)
⅓ wineglass white wine	(1)
seasoning	
6 oz. flaky pastry for the vol-au-vent case	(1 lb.)

Preparation

Peel and chop onion. Trim the kidneys, being careful to remove the white core, and chop them into smallish pieces.

Action

1. Make the flaky pastry (Appendix I) and leave to chill in the refrigerator.

2. Heat the butter and oil in a heavy saucepan, add the onions. Cover the pan and cook over a very low flame for 7 minutes.

3. When the onions are soft, but not brown, add the kidneys and cook for 5 minutes. Then add the wine and seasoning. Cover the pan again and cook over a very low heat for 30 minutes.

4. When the kidneys are cooked remove the pan from the stove and strain the juice into a jug. Transfer the kidneys to a casserole.

5. Mix the cornflour into a smooth paste with a little cold water. Return the juice to the saucepan and stir in the cornflour. Bring to the boil and cook for 2 minutes to thicken. Pour over the kidneys. Allow to cool, and chill overnight in the refrigerator.

6. Roll out the pastry to a circle of approximately 5 in. (9 in.) and $\frac{1}{2}$–$\frac{3}{4}$ in. thick. Place it on a greased baking-tray and make a circular indentation, taking care not to cut right the way through the pastry, about $\frac{1}{2}$ in. from the edge. This can be done with a smaller size flan ring, jar top, or anything else of the correct size.

7. Cook the vol-au-vent case in a hot oven for 15–20 (20–25) minutes.

8. When cooked turn on to a cake rack to cool. Before the case gets too cool, insert a sharp knife under the inner ring of pastry you made and gently lift off the top layer of pastry and reserve.

9. With your finger or a spoon, carefully scrape out any of the pastry which is at all soggy from the inside and discard. When the case is completely cold, put in an airtight tin, in which you can keep it for several days if necessary.

Next Day

Heat the vol-au-vent case and the mixture separately in the oven, and as you go into the kitchen to dish up, put the mixture in the case and replace the reserved lid.

The Day Before

Sweetbread Vol-au-Vent

½ lb. sweetbreads	(1½)
2 oz. mushrooms	(6)
1 onion	(1)
1 carrot	(1)
1 dessertspoon oil	(3)
2 oz. butter	(3)
1 heaped dessertspoon flour	(2½)
½ wineglass white wine	(1½)
¼ pint milk	(½)
1 bay leaf	(1)
1 wedge of lemon	(1)
1 sprig thyme	(1)
seasoning	
6 oz. flaky pastry	(1 lb.)

Preparation

Peel and slice onion and carrot. Remove fat from sweetbreads. Wash mushrooms and slice. Cut a wedge of lemon.

Action

1. Make the flaky pastry (Appendix I) and leave to chill in the refrigerator.

2. Place the sweetbreads in a heavy saucepan with the onion, carrot, bay leaf, thyme, lemon, seasoning and sufficient water to cover. Cover the pan and simmer gently for 15 minutes.

3. While the sweetbreads are cooking, sauté the mushrooms in the oil and ½ (1) oz. of the butter. Leave on one side.

4. Make a sauce with the remains of the butter, the flour and the milk. When the sauce has boiled for 2 minutes, withdraw the pan from the heat and stir in the wine and seasoning.

5. When the sweetbreads are cooked, drain them and add them

163

and the mushrooms to the sauce. Transfer the mixture to a casserole, cool and chill overnight in the refrigerator.

6. Roll out the pastry and cook the vol-au-vent case following the instructions given in numbers 6–9 in the recipe for Veal Kidney Vol-au-Vent.

Next Day

Heat the vol-au-vent case and the mixture separately in the oven, and as you go into the kitchen to dish up, put the mixture in the case and replace the lid.

Note: Cooked chicken could be substituted for the sweetbreads at stage 5, if preferred.

The Day Before

Colman's Crab Vol-au-Vent

8 oz. fresh or frozen crabmeat	(1½ lb.)
2 oz. mushrooms	(6)
1 small onion	(2)
1 oz. butter	(2)
1 tablespoon oil	(3)
½ cup milk	(1½)
2 tablespoons double cream	(¼ pint)
1 egg yolk	(2)
½ teaspoon dry mustard	(1 rounded)
1 dessertspoon brandy	(3)
seasoning	
6 oz. flaky pastry	(1 lb.)

Preparation

Extract any bones from the crabmeat. Wash and slice the mushrooms. Peel and finely chop the onion(s). Mix the mustard slowly with the milk, taking care not to get any lumps. Separate egg white(s) and yolk(s).

Action

1. Make the flaky pastry (Appendix I) and leave to chill in the refrigerator.

2. Heat the oil in a frying-pan with a lid, and sauté the onions in the closed pan for 10 minutes, taking care not to brown.

3. Add the mushrooms and cook for a further 5 minutes, then transfer the onions and mushrooms to a plate.

4. Add the butter to the remains of the oil and heat, then cook the crab in this for 3 (6) minutes over a high heat. Pour over the brandy, which you should first warm, and flame.

5. Return the mushrooms and onion to the pan. Stir in the milk and mustard mixture and bring to the boil. Cook for 3 minutes and season.

6. Transfer to a casserole, use 2 tablespoons of the liquid to mix with the egg yolk, then stir this in when the mixture has cooled a little. Cool, and chill overnight in the refrigerator.

7. Roll out the pastry and cook the vol-au-vent case following the instructions given in numbers 6–9 in the recipe for Veal Kidney Vol-au-Vent.

Next Day

Stir in the cream and heat the mixture and the vol-au-vent case separately in the oven, and when you go into the kitchen to dish up, put the mixture into the case and replace the reserved lid.

Afters

The Day Before

Brandy Snaps

¾ oz. golden syrup	(2)
¾ oz. butter	(2)
½ oz. castor sugar	(1½)
¾ oz. flour	(1¾)
1 pinch ginger	(¼ teaspoon)
⅛ pint double cream	(⅓)

Preparation

Grease well the handles of as many wooden spoons, or similar,
as you can, with lard, margarine or butter. You will need these
very quickly after the brandy snaps have cooked, to curl them
with. Also grease as many baking-trays as you have available.[1]

Action

1. Melt the syrup, butter and sugar in a saucepan over a low heat.

2. Remove the pan from the heat and stir in the flour, and the
   ginger.

3. Drop teaspoonsful of the mixture on to the greased baking-
   trays, at least 2 in. apart. Bake in a moderate oven for 3–4
   minutes until brown.

4. Take the trays out of the oven and allow the brandy snaps
   to cool slightly, but not harden, then roll each one round the
   handle of a greased spoon and lay them on a cake rack to set.

Next Day

Whip the cream and stuff the rolls with it.

Note: Brandy snaps do need a bit of practice and it is difficult
to achieve good results with the small quantity. As they keep very

[1] In view of the panic in the kitchen as wooden spoons go flying, we recommend in fact that you cook the brandy snaps in batches of not more than six
at a time, otherwise they may go too hard to roll.

well in airtight tins for a week or two if they are not filled with cream, we recommend using the larger quantity and eating up the inevitable broken bits over a period of time!

The Day Before

Lemon Meringue Pie

1 lemon	(2 large)
½ oz. butter	(1½)
1 egg	(3)
1 level tablespoon flour	(3)
1 level tablespoon granulated sugar	(2½)
1½ oz. castor sugar	(3)
⅛ pint water	(¼)
4½ oz. short-crust pastry	(8)

Preparation

Grate the rind from one lemon. Squeeze all the juice. Separate egg white(s) and yolk(s).

Action

1. Make the pastry (Appendix I) and roll out to line a 5–6-in. (8–9-in.) flan case. Prick the bottom of the pastry all over with a fork, and in the middle lay a sheet of greased paper or foil on which you should put a handful of uncooked rice or dried beans to stop the pastry rising. Bake in a hot oven for 30 minutes or until the pastry is lightly browned.

2. While the pastry is cooking blend the flour and water together slowly in a saucepan, bring it to the boil, stirring constantly, and once it has come to the boil cook for 2 minutes.

3. Remove the pan from the heat and stir in the butter, granulated sugar, lemon juice and rind and when it has cooled slightly, the egg yolk(s).

170

4. When the flan case is cooked, remove from oven and pour in the lemon mixture. Stiffly beat the egg white(s) and fold in the castor sugar. Spread this on top of the lemon mixture and return the flan to a low oven for 20 minutes.

5. Allow to cool and store in a cool place overnight.

The Day Before

Treacle Tart

3 tablespoons golden syrup	(8)
2 dessertspoons fresh white breadcrumbs	(6)
1 teaspoon lemon juice	(3)
4½ oz. short-crust pastry	(8)

Preparation

Make the breadcrumbs. Squeeze the lemon juice.

Action

1. Make the pastry (Appendix I). Roll it out to line a 5–6-in. (8–9-in.) flan case, but make it about ½ in. bigger all round than you need. Prick the bottom of the case all over with a fork and press the pastry down well. Cut off the excess pastry, and make it into strips which you should twist gently.

2. Sprinkle half the breadcrumbs on the bottom of the pastry case. Spoon over the golden syrup and lemon juice, and sprinkle on the rest of the breadcrumbs.

3. Arrange the twists of pastry on top to make the tart look attractive.

4. Bake in a hot oven for 15 minutes, then turn down to low for another 15 minutes. Cool and store in a cool place overnight.

Next Day

Either serve cold, or heat gently in a low oven.

The Day Before

Caramelized Citrous Liqueur

1 grapefruit	(2)
1 large orange	(4)
1 tablespoon Bols gin or kirsch	(3)

sufficient moist brown sugar to cover the fruit
    one-eighth of an inch thick

Preparation

Peel the grapefruit and oranges, removing as much of the pith as possible.

Action

1. With a sharp knife cut the segments from the inner skins of the grapefruit and oranges. Place the segments in a heat-proof dish only just large enough to hold all the fruit as it needs to come to within ½ in. of the top of the dish.

2. Pour over the Bols gin or kirsch or some other dry liqueur and stir it in. Try to arrange the fruit so that you have an even surface on top.

3. Heat your grill and when it is hot sprinkle the brown sugar over the fruit and immediately put it under a very hot grill for 2 minutes to caramelize the sugar. Chill in the refrigerator until required.

Note: If you like the idea of the caramel still being hot you can, providing you have your grill hot, sprinkle on the sugar when you go out to the kitchen after your main course, and put it under the grill then.

The Hour Before

Banana Cream

3 ripe bananas (10)
1 egg (3)
1 tablespoon brandy (3)
1 tablespoon icing-sugar (3)
1 tablespoon double cream ($\frac{1}{4}$ pint)

Preparation

Separate the egg yolk and white. Skin the bananas.

Action

1. Mash the bananas finely together with the brandy, icing-sugar and cream.

2. Stir in the egg yolk.

3. Stiffly whip the egg white and fold into the mixture. Pour the mixture into glasses and chill in the refrigerator.

The Day Before

Banana Fuzz

4 bananas (12)
1 lemon (2)
4 (approx.) tablespoons castor sugar (12)
1 pinch mixed spice ($\frac{1}{2}$ teaspoon)
$\frac{1}{3}$ cup water ($1\frac{1}{4}$)
Serve with cream

Preparation

Squeeze the lemon.

Action

1. Peel the bananas and prick them all over with a fork, then put

them in a dish with the lemon juice. Soak them in the lemon juice for 30 minutes, turning them over occasionally.

2. Drain the bananas and roll them in the castor sugar.

3. Place the bananas in a lightly-buttered fireproof dish. Sprinkle over the mixed spice and add the water.

4. Bake in a moderate oven for 30 minutes, then cool, and chill in the refrigerator until required.

Note: This dish is also good hot if you do it as an 'hour before' dish.

The Day Before

Black Cherries in Wine

½ lb. ripe black cherries	(1½)
1 wineglass red wine	(3)
1 pinch cinnamon	(¼ teaspoon)
1 clove	(2)
1 dessertspoon sugar	(3)
1 dessertspoon redcurrant jelly	(3)
1 dessertspoon brandy	(2)
½ teaspoon castor sugar to sweeten cream	(1 heaped)
⅛ pint double cream	(⅓)

Preparation

Wash cherries, remove stalks and stones.

Action

1. Put the cherries, wine, cinnamon, clove(s) and sugar in a saucepan and stew gently for about 10 minutes, or until the cherries are soft.

2. Extract the cherries from the saucepan and put into a dish to cool, but continue boiling the juice until it is reduced to half and is fairly thick in consistency.

3. When the juice has been reduced, blend in the redcurrant jelly. Remove the clove(s) and when cool, chill in the refrigerator. Also chill the cherries, but separately.

Next Day

Whip the cream with the sugar and brandy. At the point of service tip the juice over the cherries in individual glasses and top with the whipped cream.

The Day Before

Chinese Grapes

> 1 small tin lychees   (3)
> $\frac{1}{2}$ lb. large black grapes   ($1\frac{1}{2}$)
> Serve with cream

Preparation

Pip the grapes, but don't skin them unless they are very tough, as the blackness of the grapes against the whiteness of the lychees makes this dish attractive.

Action

1. Arrange the grapes and lychees, either in one big bowl, or in individual bowls, and pour over the syrup from the lychees.

2. Chill overnight in the refrigerator.

The Day Before

Caramelized Grapes

> $\frac{3}{4}$ lb. white grapes (seedless if possible)   (2)
> $\frac{1}{4}$ pint double cream   ($\frac{1}{2}$)
> 1 tablespoon sherry   (3)
> approx. 4 tablespoons moist brown sugar   (10)

Preparation

Wash and pip the grapes if not seedless. Unless they have very
tough skins it is not necessary to peel them. Whip about $\frac{1}{3}$ of the
cream. This is going to be used to make a thin layer of cream on
top of the grapes, so it will depend on what size dish you are
using.

Action

1. Put the grapes in a heat-proof dish only just large enough to
   hold all the fruit, as it needs to come to within half an inch of the
   top of the dish.
2. Pour over the unwhipped cream and sherry and stir in.
3. Put the whipped cream over the grapes as if you were icing a
   cake. Chill in the refrigerator overnight.

Next Day

Take the dish out of the refrigerator an hour before you are going
to serve it. When you come out to the kitchen to collect the main
course, turn on your grill to get really hot, and as you bring out
the plates again, sprinkle the brown sugar over the top of the
grapes and put under the grill for about 2 minutes, or until the
sugar caramelizes.

Note: Commercially soured cream or yoghourt are good substitutes for the fresh cream and sherry.

The Day Before

Grapefruit with Gin

1 grapefruit	(3)
2 dessertspoons gin	(6)

Action

1. Prepare the grapefruit in the ordinary way, but do not add any
   sugar. Pour a dessertspoon of gin over each half.

2. Chill overnight in the refrigerator.

Note: Unless you have a very sweet tooth, sugar is not necessary for the gin sweetens the grapefruit as well as giving it an interesting flavour.

The Day Before

Grapes with Grapefruit

1 fresh grapefruit   (3)
16 small grapes   (48—about 1 lb.)
2 heaped teaspoons castor sugar   (6)

Preparation

Peel and pip grapes.

Action

1. Cut the grapefruit in half, then cut out the entire fleshy part and reserve the empty shells.

2. Take all the skin and pith from the grapefruit flesh, then return the pure fruit to the shell with eight grapes per shell.

3. Sprinkle with sugar and chill in the refrigerator. It is a good idea to cover the grapefruit with foil to prevent it drying up.

The Hour Before

Mandarin Pineapple

1 small pineapple   (1 very large or 2 small)
1 small tin mandarin oranges   (1 large)
1 dessertspoon icing-sugar   (3)

Preparation

Nil.

Action

1. Cut the pineapple into the required number of portions lengthways. Then cut the flesh from the skin, but leaving it in place.
   Cut away the layer of core.

2. Divide each of the portions of pineapple into half-inch sections
   crossways, and discard the two end chunks. (Keep them for
   breakfast.)

3. Insert a mandarin segment in each section so that you end up
   with one mandarin segment and one pineapple chunk alternately.

4. At the point of service sprinkle on the icing-sugar.

The Day Before

Orange Apple Snow

2 medium cooking-apples   (6)
½ orange   (1 large or 2 small)
1 egg white   (2)
4 tablespoons castor sugar   (10)
Serve with cream

Preparation

Thinly grate the rind from the orange and squeeze the juice. Peel
the apples, core and quarter them, then slice thinly. Separate egg
white(s) and yolk(s).

Action

1. Put the apples in a saucepan with the orange peel and juice
   and the castor sugar. Cover the pan and simmer for 15
   minutes, or until the apple is soft.

2. Purée the fruit and allow to cool.

3. When the apple is cold, stiffly beat the egg white and fold it in.

178

Pour the mixture into a bowl and chill in the refrigerator until required.

The Hour Before

Orange Baked Apples

1 cooking-apple	(6)
½ orange	(2)
6 teaspoons honey	(18)
Serve with cream	

Preparation

Peel orange(s) and cut into rings, allowing two rings per apple if they are very big, or one if they are small. Cut the apple(s,) with their skin on, into three, or in half if small, across the core. Then cut out the cores.

Action

1. In a heatproof dish stand the bottom piece of the apple and fill the hole left by the core with honey.

2. Put a circle of orange on top, then another piece of apple, filling that hole with honey, and continue in this manner if you are using the large apples until all the ingredients are used up.

3. Bake the apples in a moderate oven for 1 hour.

The Day Before

Mellowed Peaches

2 large fresh ripe peaches	(6)
2 heaped dessertspoons ground almonds	(6)
1 dessertspoon brandy	(3)
1 oz. butter	(2)
2 tablespoons castor sugar	(6)
1 teaspoon lemon juice	(3)
Serve with cream	

Preparation

Skin the peaches by plunging into boiling water for 1 minute then straight into cold water. Prepare a shallow buttered fireproof dish.

Action

1. Cut the peaches in half and remove the stone. Place the halves in the buttered fireproof dish and sprinkle them with the lemon juice.

2. Mix together the almonds, butter and brandy into a paste. Divide the paste evenly between the peach halves and place it in the holes left by the removal of the stones.

3. Put $\frac{1}{2}$ tablespoon of castor sugar on top of each half peach and bake them in a moderate oven for 30 minutes. Remove from oven, allow to cool, and chill in refrigerator until required.

Note: The best peaches for this dish are the large freestone peaches.

The Day Before

Peaches in Wine

2 large fresh ripe peaches (see note above)	(6)
1 glass white wine	(3)
2 tablespoons castor sugar	(6)

Preparation

Peel the peaches by plunging for 1 minute into boiling water, then immediately into cold water.

Action

1. Cut the peaches in half and remove the stones. Place two peach halves per person in a large wineglass and cover each with a tablespoon of castor sugar.

2. Fill the wineglasses up with the white wine and place them in the refrigerator overnight.

The Hour Before

Pear Drops

2 fresh ripe dessert pears	(6)
2 teaspoons sherry	(6)
¼ pint single cream	(½)
2 heaped teaspoons sugar	(6)

Preparation

Tip the cream into a bowl.

Action

1. Peel the pears and divide them into quarters removing the core. As you peel them plunge them immediately into the bowl of cream so they become coated all over.

2. When all the pears have been coated with the cream, take them out and put 4 pieces per person into glasses. Add a teaspoon of sherry and sugar per glass, then pour over the remains of the cream used for coating.

3. Chill until ready to serve.

The Day Before
Pineapple Melon

    1 small melon (preferably honeydew)   (1 large)
    1 baby pineapple   (1 medium)
    2 tablespoons kirsch or similar liqueur   (6)

Preparation
Nil.

Action

1. Cut the top off the melon and reserve. Also shave a piece off the bottom to make the melon stand flat.

2. Remove the seeds from the melon with a spoon, then scoop out the flesh, cut it into pieces and put into a bowl.

3. Skin the pineapple, remove the core and cut the flesh into chunks. Mix with the melon, and stir in the liqueur.

4. Return the melon and pineapple to the melon shell. You may like to add a little sugar, but we personally prefer it without. Replace the top on the melon and cover the dish completely in foil before chilling in the refrigerator until required.

Note: If necessary 1 small (1 large) tin pineapple chunks could be substituted.

The Day Before
Pineapple Medley

    1 small pineapple   (1 large)
    1 small orange   (3)
    1 small apple   (2)
    1 small pear   (2)
    8 grapes   (24)
    3 tablespoons white wine (1 wineglass)
    2 tablespoons castor sugar   (6)
    Serve with cream

Preparation

Peel the orange(s), apple(s), pear(s) and grapes and remove cores
and seeds.

Action

1. Cut the top off the pineapple, preserving the leaves and put
   on one side. Carefully cut all the flesh out of the pineapple,
   taking care not to damage the shell.

2. Chop the pineapple flesh into cubes, discarding the hard central
   core. Put it into a large bowl and chop up the other fruit with
   it as though you were making a fruit salad. Add this to the
   pineapple and mix well together.

3. Sprinkle over the sugar and stir in the wine.

4. Put as much of the fruit and juice as will go into the pineapple
   shell, and arrange the rest of it in a glass bowl. Replace the
   lid on the pineapple, and cover the dish completely with foil
   before chilling in the refrigerator until required.

The Day Before

Strawberry or Raspberry Meringue Cake

½ lb. strawberries or raspberries	(1¾)
1 egg white	(4)
2 level tablespoons castor sugar	(8)
1 pinch salt	(1)
¼ pint double cream	(½)

Preparation

Hull the strawberries. Separate the egg white(s) and yolk(s).

Action

1. Beat the egg white with a pinch of salt until very stiff. Then
   beat in ½ dessertspoon (2) of the sugar. Fold in the remainder.

183

2. Pour the meringue mixture on to two sheets of oiled grease-proof paper or foil, making two equal-sized circles.

3. Bake the meringue in a very, very cool oven for 3 to 4 hours. Then allow to cool completely and store in an airtight tin.

Next Day

Whip the cream and spread it on the two meringue halves. Cut the strawberries in half, reserving four whole ones to go on the top, and put them or the raspberries in the middle of the two meringue layers, then sandwich them together. Decorate with the whole fruit.

Note: You can make meringues several days in advance and it is a good way of using up egg whites left over from mayonnaise. Store the meringues in airtight tins.

The Day Before

Orange and Apricot Cream

1 small tin of apricots	(1 large)
1 orange	(3)
⅛ pint double cream	(½)

Preparation

Wash the orange(s) and slice with the skin on.

Action

1. Put the apricots and orange(s) into a saucepan. Cover and simmer over a low heat for 20 minutes. Stir occasionally to see that the fruit isn't sticking.

2. Remove from the heat and strain any excess liquid into a jug.

3. Tip the fruit into an electric blender if you have one and mix to a smooth paste. If not, push through a coarse sieve, rejecting the orange skins.

184

4. Allow the purée to cool, and when cold add enough of the liquid to make it the consistency of thick cream.

5. Lightly whip the cream and stir in. Pour the mixture into individual glasses and chill overnight in the refrigerator.

The Day Before

Lemon Syllabub

½ large lemon	(1½)
2 tablespoons castor sugar	(6)
2 tablespoons sherry	(6)
¼ pint double cream	(¾)

Preparation

Grate the rind from the lemon and squeeze the juice.

Action

1. Whip the cream until it begins to thicken, then slowly add the sherry, lemon rind, juice and sugar. Whip again until thick.

2. Pour the mixture into syllabub glasses if you have them, otherwise wineglasses will do, and chill overnight in the refrigerator.

The Day Before

Oranged Prunes

12 large pre-cooked California prunes	(36)
1 orange	(3)
1 egg	(3)
2 tablespoons double cream	(¼ pint)
1 dessertspoon castor sugar	(3)

Preparation

Grate the rind of ½ (1½) orange(s). Skin the orange(s) and cut the flesh from the inner skins and remove pips. Stone the prunes and chop them if you have only a small blender. Separate the egg yolk(s) and white(s).

Action

1. Place the prunes, grated orange rind, orange flesh, egg yolk(s) and sugar in an electric blender and mix until smooth.

2. Whip the egg white until stiff.

3. Stir the unwhipped cream into the fruit purée, then fold in the egg white(s).

4. Pour mixture into a bowl and chill until required in the refrigerator.

Note: This is the only recipe in this book for which it is essential to have an electric mixer of some kind as it is impossible to get the purée smooth by hand.

The Day Before

Plum Orange Cream

1 large cooking apple	(3)
6 large blue plums	(18)
½ orange	(1 large)
3 tablespoons brown sugar	(9)
2 tablespoons double cream	(¼ pint)

Preparation

Peel, core and slice apple(s.) Wash plums. Finely grate the rind from the orange and squeeze the juice.

Action

1. In a heavy saucepan gently simmer the apples, plums and

sugar for 15 minutes or until the fruit is soft. Do not add any water, but stir the fruit until the juice begins to appear, then cover the pan, but do keep an eye on it.

2. When the fruit is soft, extract the stones from the plums, and if you have a blender tip the contents of the saucepan into it, together with the orange juice and grated rind and blend until smooth. If you don't have a blender, push the fruit through a sieve and extract the skins of the plums. (This is not necessary if you have a blender.) Then stir in the orange juice and rind.

3. When the purée has cooled, stir in the unwhipped cream and chill overnight in the refrigerator.

The Day Before

Apple Crumble

1 large cooking-apple	(3)
2 heaped tablespoons flour	(6)
1 oz. butter	(3)
1 dessertspoon mixed dried fruit	(2)
2 dessertspoons moist brown sugar	(6)
1 tablespoon castor sugar	(3)
Serve with cream	

Preparation

Skin, core and slice the apple(s).

Action

1. Sieve the flour into a mixing-bowl and add the butter in small pieces. Rub the two together with your fingers until you have something the consistency of breadcrumbs. Then stir in the castor sugar.

2. Put the slices of apple in a pie-dish with the mixed fruit and cover them with the moist brown sugar.

3. Sprinkle the flour and butter mixture on top of the apple, and if you want to eat the pudding cold, cook it now in a hot oven for 30 minutes, or if you want to eat it hot the following day, put it in the refrigerator overnight and cook the next day in a hot oven for 30 minutes.

Next Day

If you changed your mind mid-stream and decide you want your cold pudding hot, it will reheat perfectly well. If you haven't already cooked it, bake in a hot oven for 30 minutes.

Note: Almost any fresh fruit can be used instead of apples, and rhubarb and plums are particularly good.

The Day Before

Blackberry and Apple Summer Pudding

½ lb. fresh blackberries	(1½)
1 small cooking-apple	(2 medium)
2 tablespoons castor sugar	(6)
8 (approx.) slices *stale* white bread	(1 small loaf—24 slices approx.)
1 dessertspoon lemon juice	(3)
⅛ pint cream	(¼)

Preparation

Skin and core the apple, then slice. Slice the stale bread fairly thinly and cut off the crusts.

Action

1. Put the sliced apple, blackberries, sugar and lemon juice in a saucepan without adding any water, and simmer very gently for 15 minutes.

2. While the fruit is cooking line a bowl with the bread, reserving enough slices to form a lid.

3. When the fruit is cooked, pour it into the bread-lined bowl and put the reserved slices of bread on top, turning over the tops of the side slices of bread if the fruit does not quite reach the top.

4. Put a weighted plate on top of the pudding. Allow it to cool and put it in the refrigerator to chill, leaving the weight on top to allow the fruit juice to penetrate the bread.

Next Day

Take off the weight and loosen the pudding round the edges with a knife, and turn it out on to a plate. Whip the cream and cover the pudding with it.

Note: This pudding is also very good made traditionally with red-currants and raspberries.

The Hour Before

Bread and Plum Pudding

2 large slices of white bread	(6)
½ lb. large ripe plums	(1½)
1½ oz. butter	(4)
2 dessertspoons brown sugar	(6)
Serve with cream	

Preparation

Stone the plums and cut the crusts off the bread. Butter a shallow fireproof dish.

Action

1. Butter the bread on one side and place in the prepared dish buttered side down.

2. Place the plums on the bread and add knobs of the remaining butter. Sprinkle the plums with the sugar and cover the dish with buttered paper.

3. Bake in a moderate oven for 30 minutes.

The Day Before

Apricot Ice Cream

¾ lb. fresh apricots	(2)
1 orange	(3)
¼ pint double cream	(¾)
4 tablespoons castor sugar	(12)

Preparation

Set the refrigerator to very cold. Finely grate the rind from one orange and reserve. Peel the orange(s) and cut the segments out of the inner skins. Wash the apricots.

Action

1. Place the apricots, orange segments and sugar in a heavy saucepan and stir until the juice begins to run out of the fruit, then cover the pan and simmer for 15 minutes over a very low heat, making sure every now and then that the fruit is not sticking.

2. When the fruit is soft, remove it from the pan and extract the apricot stones. If you have a blender put the fruit and the juice in and mix until smooth. If not, press the purée through a sieve.

3. Lightly whip the cream and stir into the purée, together with the orange rind. Turn the purée into an ice tray and put in the freezing compartment of the refrigerator until hard. It is a good idea to stir the purée once or twice during freezing to prevent crystals forming, but if you don't have time it is not essential.

The Day Before

Blackcurrant Ice Cream

¾ lb. tin of blackcurrants	(2 lb.)
¼ pint double cream	(¾)

Preparation

Set refrigerator at very cold.

Action

1. Strain the blackcurrant juice into a saucepan and boil to reduce the quantity to half. Cool.

2. Put the blackcurrants in a blender if you have one and mix until smooth. If not, mash them until they are smooth.

3. Put the puréed fruit through a sieve to remove some of the pips.

4. Add the syrup to the purée. Lightly whip the cream and stir in. Pour the mixture into a freezing-tray, and put in the freezing compartment of the refrigerator until hard. It is a good idea to stir the ice cream once or twice during freezing to disperse the crystals, but it is not essential.

The Day Before

Raspberry Ice Cream

1 lb. raspberries	(3)
3 level tablespoons castor sugar	(9)
¼ pint double cream	(¾)

Preparation

Set refrigerator to very cold.

Action

1. Mash the raspberries finely, or if you have a blender put them in there to purée.

2. Stir in the sugar.

3. Lightly whip the cream and stir that into the purée.

191

4. Turn the mixture into the freezing drawer and leave in the freezing compartment of the refrigerator for 24 hours. If you can, it is a good idea to stir the fruit once or twice while it is setting to stop the crystals forming.

Note: Any soft fruit, particularly strawberries, may be substituted, though it should be noted that some fruit will need more sugar.

The Day Before

Orange Water Ice

3 oranges	(9)
½ lemon	(1 large)
4 oz. loaf sugar	(12)
½ pint water	(1½)

Preparation

Grate the rind from 1 (2) of the oranges. Squeeze the juice from the oranges and the lemon. Set refrigerator to very cold.

Action

1. Put the sugar and water in a saucepan over a low heat, stirring constantly until the sugar has dissolved. Add the lemon juice.

2. When the sugar has completely dissolved, and not before, boil the syrup for 10 minutes.

3. Stir in the orange juice and allow the mixture to cool.

4. Pour the mixture into an ice tray and freeze it for at least 12 hours. If you can, stir the mixture once or twice during the freezing time.

The Day Before

Fresh Lemon Jelly

2 large lemons	(6)
4 level tablespoons castor sugar	(12)
½ oz. gelatin	(2)
¼ pint water	(2)

Preparation

If using an electric blender, none. If not, grate the rind from half the lemons, and squeeze the juice.

Action (with blender)

1. Heat ¼ pint of the water and dissolve the gelatin in it.

2. Heat the rest of the water and dissolve the sugar in it.

3. Coarsely chop the lemons, leaving their skins on, and put the lemon chunks in the blender with the water in which the sugar is dissolved. Blend very quickly—only about 20 seconds —so that the lemon rind doesn't become too fine.

4. Strain the juice into a bowl and stir in the dissolved gelatin. Taste for sweetness, and add more sugar if necessary.

5. Pour into a mould or bowl, and leave in a cool place to set.

Action (without blender)

1. As before.

2. As before.

3. Mix thoroughly the lemon juice, grated rind, and water in which the sugar is dissolved.

4. Stir in the dissolved gelatin. Taste for sweetness, and add more sugar if necessary.

5. As before.

Note: This is very refreshing after a rich meal and it is not intended to be a very solid kind of jelly. If, however, you prefer it more solid, we recommend you add more gelatin.

The Day Before

Blackberry Mousse

6 oz. blackberries	(1 lb.)
1½ oz. castor sugar	(4)
1 dessertspoon lemon juice	(3)
1 tablespoon cold water	(3)
1 level dessertspoon powdered gelatin	(1 rounded tablespoon)
1 egg white	(2)
2 tablespoons double cream	(¼ pint)
Serve with cream	

Preparation

Squeeze the lemon juice. Separate egg yolk(s) and white(s). Wash the blackberries.

Action

1. Place the blackberries, sugar and lemon juice in a heavy saucepan and simmer gently, with the lid on the pan, for 10 minutes. At the same time put the gelatin to soak in a bowl with the water.

2. When the fruit has cooked stir in the gelatin and mix until it is completely dissolved.

3. Sieve the fruit to make a purée, pushing through as much of it as possible, but discarding the pips. Cool.

4. When the fruit purée is just beginning to set, whisk the egg white(s) until stiff, and the cream. Fold both into the purée. Pour into individual glasses or a bowl and chill until required.

The Day Before
Chocolate Mousse

2 oz. bitter chocolate	(6)
2 eggs	(6)
3 level tablespoons castor sugar	(9)
1 tablespoon brandy	(3)
2 dessertspoons water	(6)

Preparation

Separate egg yolks and whites.

Action

1. Melt the chocolate, water and sugar in a saucepan over a low heat until completely dissolved. Remove the pan from the heat and beat in the egg yolks one at a time.

2. Stir in the brandy and leave cooling while you whip the egg whites until stiff.

3. Fold in the egg whites and mix thoroughly.

4. Pour the mixture into individual glasses and chill in the refrigerator until required.

The Day Before
Honey Mousse

2 tablespoons honey	(6)
2 small eggs	(4 large)
⅛ pint double cream	(⅓)

Preparation

Separate the egg whites and yolks. Whip the cream.

Action

1. Whip the egg yolks and the honey together in a bowl. Then put

195

the bowl over a pan of boiling water and keep stirring the eggs and honey until they thicken. Do not let them boil though.

2. Remove the mixture from the heat when thickened and allow to cool. Meanwhile whip the egg whites until stiff.

3. When the mixture has cooled, stir in the cream and finally fold in the egg whites.

4. Pour the mixture into individual dishes or glasses and chill until required.

Note: This is an extremely sweet pudding!

The Day Before

Lemon Mousse

1 large lemon	(3)
2 small eggs	(6)
2 dessertspoons castor sugar	(6)
$\frac{1}{8}$ pint double cream	$(\frac{1}{3})$
1 heaped teaspoon gelatin	(3)
1 tablespoon water	(3)

Preparation

Grate the rind from $\frac{1}{2}$ (1) lemon. Separate the egg white and egg yolks. Squeeze the lemon juice.

Action

1. Dissolve the gelatin in the water in a small bowl, and put it in a larger bowl of hot water to melt completely.

2. In a separate bowl, over a pan of very hot water, place the sugar, grated lemon rind and the egg yolks. Whisk until frothy, then take the bowl off the pan.

3. Add to the egg yolks, etc. the lemon juice and gelatin and beat until well blended.

4. Leave this mixture until the gelatin has begun to set. Meantime, whip the cream, and stiffly beat the egg whites.

5. When the mixture has almost set, fold in the cream and egg whites. Turn into a soufflé dish and chill in the refrigerator until required.

Next Day

Decorate as required.

The Day Before

Creamed Rice

1½ tablespoons pudding (Carolina) rice	(4)
½ pint creamy milk	(1¼)
1 tablespoon castor sugar	(3)
1 pinch salt	(1)
1 pinch nutmeg	(1)
2 dessertspoons double cream	(¼ pint)

Preparation

Thoroughly wash the rice.

Action

1. Put all the ingredients, except the cream, into a pie dish and cook in a slow oven for 2 (2½) hours, or until the rice is soft but not soggy.

2. Allow to cool, remove skin, and stir in the double cream.

3. Chill until required.

The Day Before

Ginger Brandy

9 gingernut biscuits	(24)
¼ pint double cream	(⅔)
4 tablespoons brandy	(12)

Preparation

Whip the cream and put enough of it into the refrigerator to use to decorate the pudding next day.

Action

1. Sprinkle the gingernuts with the brandy and place some of them in a small (medium) dish and cover with some of the cream. Continue with alternate layers of gingernuts and cream until all ingredients are used up, finishing with a gingernut layer. Put a weighted plate on top of the gingernuts and chill overnight in the refrigerator.

Next Day

Decorate the top of the pudding with the cream you reserved.

The Day Before

Orange and Almond Pudding

1 large orange	(3)
1½ oz. ground almonds	(4)
¾ oz. fresh white breadcrumbs	(2)
4 level tablespoons castor sugar	(12)
2 small eggs	(4 standard)
Serve topped with whipped cream	

Preparation

Make the breadcrumbs. Grate the rind from one of the oranges and squeeze each one. Separate the egg white(s) and yolks.

Action

1. Beat the egg yolks and sugar together in a fairly large bowl until creamy.

2. Stir in the breadcrumbs, almonds, orange juice and rind.

3. Stiffly beat the egg whites and fold in.

4. Pour the mixture into a buttered soufflé dish and bake in a moderate oven for 40 (55) minutes.

5. Remove from oven and allow to cool slightly before tipping out on to a cake rack. Store overnight in a cool place.

Next Day

Whip the cream and pile on top.

The Day Before

Embalmed Macaroons

4 large macaroons	(12)
¼ lb. plain cooking chocolate	(10 oz.)
2 oz. butter	(5)
2 oz. castor sugar	(5)
1 egg yolk	(2)
2 tablespoons brandy	(5)
½ cup milk	(1)
1 tablespoon water	(2)
Serve with cream.	

Preparation

Scald the milk and allow it to cool. Separate the eggs.

Action

1. Melt the chocolate in a saucepan with the water over a low heat.

2. Mix the egg yolk with the scalded milk, then stir it into the chocolate.

3. Cream together the butter and sugar, then stir it into the chocolate mixture until it is quite smooth.

4. Divide the macaroons into pieces and soak them in the brandy.

5. Arrange layers of macaroons and chocolate mixture in a dish and chill overnight in the refrigerator.

Next Day

Decorate with whipped cream.

The Day Before

Winter Trifle

3 individual sponge cakes	(8)
2 dessertspoons shredded almonds	(6)
2 tablespoons apricot jam	(6)
2 fresh tangerines	(6)
4 tablespoons sherry	(12)
$\frac{1}{8}$ pint double cream	($\frac{1}{3}$)

Preparation

Peel the tangerines and cut the segments out of their inner skins, then squeeze the empty inner skins to get out any remaining juice.

Action

1. Sprinkle half the almonds over the bottom of a bowl.

2. Split the sponge cakes in half. Spread the jam on each half. Put equal quantities of the tangerines on each half, then sandwich them together again.

200

3. Arrange the sponge cakes on top of the almonds and pour over the sherry and any juice left from the tangerines.

4. Put the remains of the almonds on top of the sponge cakes.

5. Whip the cream and cover the sponge cakes.

6. Chill in the refrigerator, or keep in a cool place until required.

The Day Before

Crème Brûlée

½ pint double cream   (1½)
1 teaspoon castor sugar   (1 tablespoon)
2 egg yolks   (6)
1–2 drops vanilla essence   (4–6)
2 tablespoons (approx.) castor sugar   (8)
    for caramelizing top

Preparation

Separate egg whites and yolks.

Action

1. Heat a pan of water and in a bowl over the pan, stir continually the cream and teaspoon (tablespoon) castor sugar until warm.

2. Beat the egg yolks until light and stir in the heated cream and vanilla essence. Pour into a soufflé dish or individual ramikins.

3. Stand the dish or dishes in a pan of water coming two-thirds of the way up the sides and bake in a moderate oven for 40 minutes in the case of the individual dishes and a little longer in the case of the large size single dish. Test with a knife blade towards end of cooking time; if it comes out clean, the cream is ready.

4. Allow to get completely cold (leave overnight if possible) then sprinkle the top of the cream with castor sugar to a depth of approximately ⅛ in.

5. Caramelize the sugar under a really hot grill, watching it carefully all the time and turning the dish or dishes if necessary so that the top is browned evenly. When caramelized, the sugar on top should be like thin ice.

6. Chill in the refrigerator until required.

The Day Before

Zabaglione

2 egg yolks	(6)
2 level tablespoons castor sugar	(6)
2 tablespoons sherry	(6)
1 level teaspoon gelatin	(1 level dessertspoon)
1 tablespoon boiling water	(1½)

Preparation

Separate the eggs. Mix the gelatin and water and dissolve as much as possible.

Action

1. Place all the ingredients in a double saucepan, or a bowl over very hot water, and whisk until the mixture becomes thick and fluffy.

2. Pour the mixture into individual glasses and chill overnight in the refrigerator.

Note: Be sure to go on whisking long enough, otherwise you will find that as soon as the mixture gets cold it will separate. If you decide to serve the Zabaglione warm in the traditional way immediately after making it, there is no need to include the gelatin and water.

Appendices

APPENDIX I
GENERAL INSTRUCTIONS
Pastry

The art of successful pastry making is to keep everything as cool as possible and to handle it no more than is necessary.

When covering a pie, you want to roll the pastry out to about ½ in. wider all round than you need it. Cut off this surplus. Wet the rim of the pie-dish and make an edge all round the dish with the surplus pastry. Wet this again, then carefully pick up the main pastry, balancing it with the rolling-pin, and put it on top of the spare rim. Press the two pieces of pastry together, then hold up the pie-dish and cut round the edge (from the bottom) with a knife. With the pastry that is left over you can make squirls or whatever you like to go on top. You should always make an incision in the pie top somewhere, to allow the steam to escape. Brushing pastry with a raw egg will give it a glazed look and it also helps to prevent it going soggy.

To Make Short-Crust Pastry

The ingredients are flour, fat, a pinch of salt and a little cold water. For short-crust pastry you need to allow half the quantity of fat to flour. Therefore if you have 8 oz. flour, you will need 4 oz. fat. The fat can be either half lard and half margarine or butter, or if you want a very rich pastry it can be all butter.

Action

1. Sieve the flour into a bowl. Add the salt and the fat. Cut the fat into pieces with your knife to avoid handling.

2. With the thumbs and finger-tips rub the fat into the flour until the mixture resembles breadcrumbs.

3. Add the cold water, a few drops at a time and mix with a knife. You will need approximately 3 tablespoons of water per half pound of flour. When the mixture is just damp enough to stick together, you will have the right consistency, and you can now put it on a floured board and roll out to the desired shape.

To Make Flaky Pastry

The ingredients are flour, fat, a pinch of salt, ½ teaspoon lemon juice per half pound of flour, and a little cold water.

For flaky pastry you need to allow three-quarters the quantity of fat to flour. Therefore if you have 8 oz. flour you will need 6 oz. fat. This is usually half lard and half margarine or butter.

Action

1. On a plate, thoroughly mix together the margarine and the lard and then divide it into four equal portions.

2. Sieve the flour into the bowl with a pinch of salt.

3. Put a quarter of the fat into the bowl with the flour and rub it in with the thumbs and tips of the fingers.

4. Add the lemon juice and the water a little at a time until you get an elastic paste, mixing all the time with a knife.·

5. Put the paste on to a floured board, roll it out in the shape of a long rectangle, and mark it lightly with a knife into three equal parts.

6. Put blobs of the second portion of fat on to the first two-thirds you have marked out on the pastry. Fold the pastry over in thirds and press down the edges with the rolling-pin. Turn the pastry half-way round to the left and roll it out again into the rectangle.

7. Mark the pastry into three again and repeat the procedure with the third quarter of the fat. Turn it again half-way to the left and roll out as before.

8. Repeat the procedure with the last quarter of the fat, turning it half-way to the left again.

9. When all the fat is used up, roll the pastry out once more, mark it into three and fold it without the addition of anything. Seal the edges, then do not roll out, but put the pastry as it is into the refrigerator for a few hours.

10. After you have left the pastry for a minimum of two hours, roll it out into the desired shape.

To Make a White Sauce

The ingredients are butter, flour, milk or some other liquid (if warmed it is better but not essential), and seasoning.

Action

1. Heat the butter in a saucepan large enough to hold the total quantity of liquid being used.

2. When the butter has melted, but not browned, withdraw the pan from the heat and stir in the flour. Return to the heat and cook the roux over a low heat for 2 minutes, stirring all the time.

3. Withdraw the pan from the heat again and mix in the liquid very slowly stirring all the time to avoid lumps.

4. When all the liquid is blended, return the pan to the heat and bring gently to the boil, stirring constantly.

5. Once the sauce has come to the boil, continue cooking gently and stirring for 4 minutes as it thickens, then withdraw the pan from the heat and stir in the seasoning and anything else, such as cheese, that may need to be added.

Note: The thickness of the sauce depends on the ratio of fat and flour to liquid. Therefore, to get a very thick sauce you will need less liquid proportionately to fat and flour; whereas to get a thin sauce you will need more. For a very thin sauce the quantities are

1 oz. butter, 1 oz. flour to 1 pint liquid; for a slightly thicker one, 2 oz. butter, 2 oz. flour to 1 pint liquid; and for a thick sauce 3 oz. butter, 3 oz. flour to 1 pint liquid.

If by chance you find yourself with a lumpy looking sauce, whisk it furiously just before it comes to the boil—once it has boiled it is too late, and then the only thing to do is sieve it, which is not as satisfactory as some of the goodness is lost.

To Make Mayonnaise
(By hand)

The ingredients for an average quantity of mayonnaise are: 2 egg yolks, 1 level teaspoon French mustard, pinch of salt, ½ level teaspoon castor sugar, plenty of black pepper, ½ pint olive oil, 2–3 teaspoons wine vinegar.

Action

1. Put the egg yolks into a bowl and add the French mustard, the salt, sugar and freshly ground black pepper. Mix well together.

2. Measure the oil out into a jug and add it to the egg yolks drop by drop, beating all the time until it begins to thicken. After this it may be added a little faster, but not much, otherwise the mayonnaise will curdle (a good method is to let the oil trickle *very* gently down the side of the bowl). Should this happen, break another egg yolk into a fresh bowl and mix with a little French mustard, then gradually beat the thin mayonnaise into the yolk.

3. When the oil is all used up and the mayonnaise is really thick, add a little of the vinegar to thin it to the right consistency. Adjust seasoning if necessary.

Note: Mayonnaise will keep in a screw-top jar in the refrigerator for at least a week.

To Make Mayonnaise
(With an electric liquidizer)

The ingredients for this type of mayonnaise are slightly different in that you can use one whole egg, rather than two egg yolks; otherwise they are the same.

Action

1. Put the whole egg into the liquidizer with the sugar, seasoning, mustard and vinegar. Switch on to fast, and mix.
2. Keeping the liquidizer switched to fast, pour the oil in, in a thin stream. Immediately it starts to thicken add the rest of the oil more quickly.
3. If, when all the oil is used up, the mayonnaise appears to be too thick, add a little more vinegar.

Note: In some of the recipes given, only a tablespoon or so of mayonnaise is required and it would be uneconomic to make it specially in each case. If home-made mayonnaise isn't available we suggest you use one of the proprietary brands. We mustn't recommend a particular brand, so choose the one you find has the best flavour.

To Make a Plain French Salad Dressing

The classical recipe for French dressing is 3 parts oil to 1 part vinegar, a good pinch of salt and freshly ground black pepper. However, most people have their own variations on this recipe, and two of ours are given below.

French dressing keeps well in a bottle in the refrigerator, and it is often useful to have some on hand, and we therefore recommend that you make fairly large quantities at a time.

French Dressing Number One

Five parts oil to one part wine vinegar, 1 clove of garlic, ½ teaspoon made mustard, 1 teaspoon sugar. The ingredients other than the oil and vinegar would be sufficient for 1 cup, but alter it to suit your own taste. (The thing about French dressing is that it is very much a matter of personal taste, so we suggest you experiment.) Mix together the mustard, sugar and oil, then stir in the vinegar, salt and pepper. Transfer to a screw-top bottle and put the peeled whole clove of garlic into the dressing and leave for 24 hours for the flavour to develop.

French Dressing Number Two

Four parts oil to one part wine vinegar, 1 clove garlic, 1 tablespoon each of finely chopped parsley, tarragon, chervil and chives, seasoning. Chop the herbs and garlic finely. Combine with the oil, add the vinegar and salt and freshly ground black pepper.

Another good salad dressing to make a change from mayonnaise or French dressing is a sour cream one. For this you need 4 tablespoons commercially soured cream, 2 tablespoons vinegar, or lemon juice, salt and pepper, 1 dessertspoon chopped chives, and 1 tablespoon sugar. Mix together and add more sugar to taste.

You might also like to try crumbled blue cheese in the above recipe in place of the chives. In this case, cut down on the sugar a bit.

Seasoned Flour

This is used for coating meat before frying. When a recipe calls for you to make seasoned flour, it means that you should mix with the flour, salt and pepper, and any of the herbs recommended for the particular recipe. The easiest and least messy way of coating meat in seasoned flour is to put the flour in a large polythene bag, drop the meat into it and shake the bag until the meat is completely coated with the flour.

Stock

With the exception of the recipes given in this book calling for a

Court Bouillon, stock made with a chicken or meat cube can be substituted for the real thing for which recipes are given below. However, if you are doing a lot of cooking, it is well worth having a 'stock pot'. Good stock will keep in a very cool place up to a week, but in warm weather it is necessary to boil it up every two days.

Chicken Stock

To the bones and carcass of a cooked chicken, with giblets if available, add 1 sliced carrot, 2 sticks celery, 1 onion stuck with 3 cloves, parsley, thyme and bay leaf tied together, a wedge of lemon, 1 teaspoon salt, 6 peppercorns, and 1½ pints water. Put all the ingredients in a heavy saucepan, bring to the boil and skim off the scum. Turn the heat down to low, cover the pan and simmer for 2 hours. When the stock has cooked for 2 hours, strain it into a bowl. Allow to cool and remove any fat before using.

Meat Stock

To 2–3 lb. of meat bones (these can be beef, lamb, veal, or pork, but probably the best are beef and veal), add 4 stalks celery, 2 onions stuck with 4 cloves, 1 sliced carrot, parsley, thyme and bay leaf tied together, 2 teaspoons salt, 8 peppercorns, 2–3 pints water. Put all the ingredients in a heavy saucepan, bring to the boil and skim off the scum. Turn the heat down to low, cover the pan and simmer for 2½–3 hours. When the stock is cooked, strain it into a bowl. Allow to cool and remove any fat before using.

Court Bouillon

To 2 pints water add half pound sliced carrots, 1 medium sliced onion, 1 bay leaf, 1 sprig thyme, 1 teaspoon salt, 6 tablespoons wine vinegar, 4 stalks of parsley, 6 peppercorns. Put all the ingredients, except the peppercorns, which go in 10 minutes before the end of cooking, into a saucepan. Simmer for 1 hour, adding the peppercorns at the appropriate time. Strain the liquid into a bowl when cooked.

211

APPENDIX II

VEGETABLES THAT CAN BE PREPARED IN ADVANCE OR BE COOKED AND LEFT IN THE OVEN WITHOUT HARM

Aubergines in Cheese Sauce

Peel and slice large aubergines. Cover them with salt in a colander for 30 minutes and leave with a weighted plate on top to remove excess bitterness. Boil them in salted water until soft. Make a thick cheese sauce. Place the aubergines and cheese sauce in layers in a casserole. Top with fresh white breadcrumbs and dot with butter. Heat in the oven.

Bubble and Squeak

Peel, slice and crisply fry one medium-sized onion per person. Add to the onion equal quantities of left-over mashed potatoes and cabbage or brussels sprouts, and fry until the potato is brown. Transfer to a heatproof dish and leave in a low oven until you are ready to eat.

White Cabbage, Onion and Tinned Tomatoes

Put a tablespoonful of oil per person in a saucepan. Wash, slice and chop the onions and cabbage and fry the onion in the oil with a lid on the pan for 7 minutes. Add the cabbage and cook for a further 15 minutes over a moderate heat, taking care not to let the vegetables burn. Finally, add the tinned tomatoes, transfer to a casserole and heat thoroughly. This dish can be re-heated on several occasions successfully.

Braised Celery

Thoroughly scrub the celery, then put in a casserole with a good-sized piece of butter and crumble over it a meat cube. Cover the dish and cook in a very moderate oven for 1 hour.

Braised Leeks

Soak the leeks in cold salt water for as long as possible before cooking, then they are done in the same way as celery, but will take a little longer. If you are in a hurry, do them as the recipe for braised onions given below.

Braised Onions

Peel large onions. Put them in a pan of salt water and bring them to the boil, then cook for 2 minutes. Drain them and put them in a casserole with some butter and crumble a meat cube over the top. Cover the dish and bake in a very moderate oven for 1 hour.

Braised Endive

Wash the endives and remove the outer leaves. Place in a buttered casserole, with some freshly ground black pepper. Dot with more butter. Cover tightly and bake in a moderate oven for about 35 minutes or until tender. At the point of service squeeze on a little lemon juice.

Braised Parsnips or Turnips

Peel the parsnips or turnips and cook as for Braised Onions.

Baked Tomatoes

Cut the tomatoes in half and sprinkle with sugar, seasoning and herbs if liked. Add a good knob of butter to each half. Put them in a shallow fireproof dish and bake in a low to moderate oven for 15 minutes. They should be cooked in this time, but won't deteriorate if you switch the oven down and leave longer.

Baked Tomatoes and Onions

Put layers of peeled tomatoes and peeled onions in a greased fireproof dish. Season each layer and add a little sugar to the tomato layers. Bake in a moderate oven for 1 hour. If liked, a few breadcrumbs and grated cheese can be sprinkled on top.

Baked Carrots in Foil

Wash, and peel if necessary, the carrots. Slice them and lay them on a sheet of buttered foil. Season well and make a parcel of the foil. Lay the parcel in a shallow heatproof dish and bake in a moderate oven for about 35 minutes or until the carrots are tender. To serve, tip into a dish with the juices.

Baked Courgettes in Foil with Rosemary

Wash the courgettes and peel 3 or 4 thin strips of skin from each and rub in salt, pepper and a little rosemary. Lay the courgettes on a sheet of foil and dab with butter. Make a parcel with the foil and lay in a shallow heatproof dish and bake in a moderate oven for about 35 minutes or until the courgettes are tender. Serve as for Baked Carrots.

Baked Onions in Foil

Peel and then proceed as for Baked Carrots in foil, but they will take about 45 minutes to cook in a moderate oven.

Baked Parsnips or Turnips in Foil

Peel and then proceed as for Baked Onions. These will take about 45 minutes to cook in a moderate oven.

Baked Fennel in Foil

Cut the fennel bulb into three, put in cold salted water, bring to the boil and cook for 3 minutes. Transfer to a sheet of foil, dot with butter and season with salt and pepper. Make a parcel with the foil and bake in a shallow heatproof dish in a moderate oven for about 30 minutes. Serve as for baked carrots in foil. Fennel is particularly good with a very rich dish.

Baked Aubergine and Tomatoes

Dice aubergine, cover with salt in a colander and leave for 30 minutes with a weighted plate on top to remove excess bitterness. Rinse and dry then sauté the diced aubergine in some oil. Peel and finely chop onions and sauté with the aubergines until brown. Add about a tablespoon of tinned tomatoes per person and simmer for 2 minutes. Butter a shallow fireproof dish. Add mixture and top with breadcrumbs. Dot with butter and bake in a moderate oven for 1 hour.

214

Carrot and Brussels Sprouts Casserole

Scrape fairly large carrots and slice about the thickness of a penny. Prepare brussels sprouts in the usual way. Butter a casserole and put the carrots and brussels sprouts in it in layers, seasoning each layer with salt and pepper and a little sugar. Cover and bake in a moderate oven for about 40 minutes or until the vegetables are tender (old carrots will take longer).

Turnips in a Cheese Sauce

Peel and slice turnips and boil in salt water for 15 minutes. Make a strong cheese sauce in sufficient quantity to coat the turnips. Butter a shallow baking-dish, drain the turnips and put them in the dish. Cover with the sauce and top with Parmesan cheese. This dish will keep in a very moderate oven for 1 hour.

Spinach in a Cheese Sauce

Wash spinach and boil in salted water for 10 minutes. Drain thoroughly and coarsely chop. Make a strong cheese sauce using 2 oz. butter, 1 dessertspoon flour, 2 oz. strong English cheese, 1 tablespoon Parmesan, and $\frac{1}{4}$ pint milk per each $\frac{3}{4}$ lb. spinach. When you have made the cheese sauce allow it to cool a little and stir in an egg yolk, and the spinach. Butter a casserole and put in the mixture and sprinkle with nutmeg. Bake for up to 1 hour in a very moderate oven.

Puréed Vegetables

Most vegetables such as cabbage, brussels sprouts, turnips, parsnips, and swedes, may be cooked by boiling in salt water until soft, then puréed, and mixed with butter and freshly ground black pepper. They should then be put into a casserole and they can be heated as necessary, or left for up to an hour in a low oven.

Potatoes

1. *Potatoes Baked in the Jackets*

   Scrub a medium baking potato per person, rub a little oil into them, and cook in a moderate oven for 1 hour. They will cook a little more quickly if you put them on a skewer.

215

2. *New Potatoes Baked in Foil*

If the potatoes are really small and have only a very thin skin, just wash them, but if they are a bit coarse it is better to scrape them. Having prepared them, lay them on a sheet of foil, dot with butter and sprinkle with plenty of pepper and salt. Make a parcel of the foil and put in a shallow heatproof dish and cook in a moderate oven for about 35 minutes. To serve open up the parcel and tip the potatoes into a dish with the juices.

3. *Potatoes with Cheese (Soufflé Potatoes)*

For a pound of potatoes you need 1 clove garlic, salt, pepper, freshly grated nutmeg, 1 oz. grated cheese, 1 egg, ½ pint milk, and a little extra cheese. Peel the potatoes and slice very thinly. Butter a heatproof dish and spread round it very finely peeled and chopped garlic. Put in the potatoes in layers, seasoning each as you do so with salt, pepper, cheese and nutmeg. Beat the egg and bring the milk to the boil. Pour a little of the milk on to the egg yolk and mix, then tip into the rest of the milk. Pour over the potatoes, and sprinkle on a bit more grated cheese. Dot with butter and bake in a moderate oven for about 45 minutes or until the potatoes are cooked.

4. *Layered Potatoes with Stock (Scalloped Potatoes)*

For a pound of potatoes you will also need ¼ pint chicken stock and ½ oz. butter. Peel the potatoes and cut into thin slices. Butter a casserole and put the potatoes in it in layers, seasoning each as you do so. Pour round the stock and bake in a moderate oven for about 50 minutes or until the potatoes are cooked.

5. *Potatoes with Mushrooms and Olives*

For 1 lb. of potatoes you will also need ½ a small onion, 5 stuffed olives, 2 oz. mushrooms, 1½ oz. butter, ¼ cup milk. Peel and boil the potatoes, then mash. Sauté the onion until soft but not brown. Slice the olives and mushrooms. Mix all the ingredients together and season. Butter a heatproof dish and put the mixture in it and dot with more butter. This dish will keep in a very moderate oven for an hour or more.

6. *Mashed Potatoes*

The most successful way of mashing potatoes is to peel and slice the potatoes and cook in salted water until soft. Drain the potatoes and return to the pan. Mash them with about ¼ pint milk per 1–1½ lb. potatoes, pepper, salt and 1½ oz. butter. You will find that it is easier to get rid of the lumps by mashing the potatoes over a very low heat. If you have any cream available, mix in 1 tablespoon at the end. Mashed potatoes will keep well in a low oven in a covered dish for up to 1 hour.

7. *Roast Potatoes*

The most successful way of roasting potatoes is to peel them and parboil them in salted water. Drain them and roll them in seasoned flour. Put into a baking-tray with some fat or olive oil which has been preheated, and cook in a moderately hot oven for about 40 minutes. Baste occasionally and turn the potatoes so that they get well browned and crisped on all sides.

Salads

(a) SUMMER SALADS

Mixed Summer Salad

This should include lettuce, peeled and sliced tomatoes and cucumber, sliced hard-boiled egg, spring onions and radishes, arranged attractively in a salad bowl and served with a choice of mayonnaise or French dressing.

Tomato Salad

Peel and slice the tomatoes, put in a shallow dish and sprinkle with sugar and a little salt, and plenty of freshly ground black pepper. Add a few chopped chives or very finely-chopped onion, and dress with olive oil.

Cucumber Salad

Peel and slice the cucumber very finely. (The easiest way to do this is with a potato-peeler.) Lay the cucumber slices in a shallow dish and grind some black pepper over it. Dress with vinegar.

Green Salad

This should include 2 varieties of crisp lettuce, such as Webbs Wonderful and Cos, thinly-sliced and peeled cucumber, and watercress, and be dressed with a French dressing to which herbs could be added if liked. Also if liked, tiny croûtons of bread fried in garlic butter can be sprinkled over the other ingredients.

Potato Salad

Potato salad can be made at any time of the year, but as it is so much better made with new potatoes, it is, strictly speaking, a summer salad. Scrape; and boil the new potatoes in salted water until they are just cooked. Drain and dice the potatoes. While they are still warm stir in about 1 dessertspoon mayonnaise per 2–3 new potatoes, and a teaspoon chopped chives. Put into a glass bowl and chill until required.

(b) WINTER SALADS

In winter when it is not easy to get crisp lettuce, and other traditional salad ingredients are at a premium, there are a number of substitutes you can use and we give in this section a few you might like to try.

Celeriac and Sea-Kale Salad

Allow per person, 1 small root celeriac and $\frac{1}{4}$ lb. sea-kale. Peel and slice the celeriac into sticks. Boil in salted water for 10 minutes or until tender. Wash and chop the sea-kale and boil in salted water for 7 minutes. Drain both and mix together. Cool and chill in the refrigerator. Next day dress with French dressing and sprinkle over freshly chopped parsley.

Orange and Beetroot Salad

Allow per person 3 oz. beetroot, 1 dessertspoon lemon juice, $\frac{1}{2}$ tablespoon vinegar, 1 tablespoon oil, 1 tablespoon orange juice, $\frac{1}{4}$ teaspoon orange peel, pinch salt, $\frac{1}{4}$ teaspoon grated onion, $\frac{1}{4}$ teaspoon sugar, 1–2 drops Tabasco sauce, 1 small orange and $\frac{1}{2}$ endive. Boil, cool, peel the beetroot and slice. Grate the onion and the peel from the orange. Slice $\frac{1}{2}$ of the flesh from the orange and squeeze the juice from it. Mix the lemon juice, vinegar, orange juice and peel, onion, salt, sugar and Tabasco sauce. Pour this mixture over the beetroot and put in the refrigerator to marinate for at least three hours. Peel and slice the rest of the orange and cut into thin circles. Wash and cut the endive into circles and place as a bed in a serving-dish. Drain the marinating juices from the beetroot and mix with the oil. Arrange sliced beetroot and orange alternately on the bed of endive and pour over the dressing.

Mixed Winter Salad

This should include sliced endive, celery, peeled tomatoes, shredded chicory, and shredded white cabbage, and be dressed with a French dressing.

Cabbage and Green Pepper Salad

Allow per person half a green pepper, 3 tablespoons shredded white cabbage and 1 dessertspoon large sultanas. Wash all the vegetables, deseed green pepper and chop. Chop the cabbage and mix all ingredients together and dress with a French dressing.

Aubergine and Tomato Salad

Allow per person 1 aubergine, 2 tomatoes, $\frac{1}{4}$ cup oil, pinch salt. Slice the tops off the tomatoes and scoop out the seeds. Slice the aubergine lengthways and grill for 10 minutes, or until soft. Scoop out the flesh and purée with the oil and salt. Fill the tomatoes with the purée and chill.

Cucumber and Tarragon Salad

Allow per person $\frac{1}{4}$ cucumber, $\frac{1}{2}$ celery heart, 1 tablespoon Parmesan cheese, $\frac{1}{4}$ teaspoon dried chervil, $\frac{1}{2}$ bunch watercress, $\frac{1}{4}$ cup oil, 1 tablespoon tarragon vinegar, 1 teaspoon lemon juice, and seasoning. Peel and dice the cucumber and celery. Mix with the cheese and chervil. Make a dressing with the other ingredients. Lay the cucumber and celery on a bed of watercress and spoon over the dressing.

Apple, Celery and Walnut Salad

Allow per person 1 small eating apple, 2 sticks celery, 6 peeled walnuts, 1 tablespoon mayonnaise. Peel, core and dice the apple. Skin and dice the celery. Shell and chop walnuts. Mix all together and moisten with mayonnaise.

Rice, Prawns and Nut Salad

Allow 2 tablespoons cooked rice, 1 oz. peeled prawns, 1 tablespoon cooked green peas, 1 dessertspoon peanuts per person. Mix all together, season well and moisten with French dressing.

Tomato and Endive Salad

Allow 1 stick endive and 1 large tomato per person. Skin and slice the tomatoes. Wash and chop the endive. Mix together and sprinkle over a little castor sugar. Season well and dress with French dressing.

Avocado Pear and Grapefruit Salad

Allow per person ½ avocado pear and ½ grapefruit. Cut the avocado pear in two, remove the stone, scoop the flesh out and cut into slices. Peel grapefruit and cut the segments out of the inner skins. Arrange slices of grapefruit and avocado pear alternately, perhaps on a bed of lettuce, and pour over a little French dressing. Do not cut the avocado pears more than an hour before you are going to eat as they will go brown.

Fennel Salad

Wash a fennel bulb per person. Cut into thin strips and dress with a mixture of oil, salt and lemon, allowing about 1 teaspoon oil, 1 dessertspoon lemon juice, and a pinch of salt per bulb.

Tomatoes Stuffed with Spicy Avocado

See page 50 in starter section for spicy avocado. Peel 1 large tomato per person, scrape out the seeds and stuff with the avocado mixture.

Raw Mushroom Salad

See page 54 in starter section.

Ratatouille

See page 56 in starter section.

APPENDIX III

SUPPERS AT SHORT NOTICE

For those occasions when you rashly invite friends to a meal without much thought for your larder, we have included a section on dishes which can be made at short notice after the shops have closed, using the ingredients listed in 'Storecupboard Standbys' below.

Recipes using pastry are really only possible 'at short notice' if you are a skilful pastry-maker or can buy frozen pastry in plenty of time for it to thaw.

Some of these dishes appeared earlier in the book, but other recipes are given in full on the following pages. The recipes are divided into four sections: Eggs, Fish, Miscellaneous and Desserts, and you will be able to see at a glance the ingredients required, and the amount of time involved from the start of the preparation to the time of eating. The quantities can easily be adapted for any numbers.

Storecupboard Standbys

Perishables	*Tins*
Eggs	Le-Ka-Ri Mild Malayan Curry
Bacon	Prawns
Butter	Sardines
Milk (or tin of instant or dried)	Tuna Fish
Cheddar and Parmesan Cheese	Sweetcorn or Mexicorn
Flour	Artichoke Hearts
Bread	Cream
Potatoes (and packet of instant)	Consommé and any other soups you like

Perishables	*Tins*
Squeezy Lemon Juice	Curry Powder
Onions	Tomatoes
Bar of Cooking Chocolate	Mushrooms
	Fruit
	Tongue
	Crab
	Golden Syrup

Miscellaneous

Rice
Dehydrated Peas and any other vegetables
Olive Oil
Vinegar
Herbs
Castor sugar
Moist brown sugar
Salad Cream
Tomato Ketchup
Cooking Brandy and Sherry

1. Basically Eggs
(Recipes already given)

(*a*) *Scrambled Prawns* (page 28)

Time necessary before eating: 10 minutes. Ingredients required: Prawns (use tinned as substitute), eggs, butter.

(*b*) *Egg Cutlets* (page 65)

Time necessary before eating: 45 minutes. Ingredients required: Eggs, bacon, chives (use a little grated onion as substitute), butter, flour, milk, and bread for breadcrumbs (or ready-made packet).

(*c*) *Egg and Tomato Crumble* (page 64)

Time necessary before eating: 40 minutes. Ingredients required: Eggs, tomatoes (use tinned as substitute), onion, butter, cheese, sugar, bread for breadcrumbs.

(*d*) *Egg, Bacon and*   Time necessary before eating: 50 minutes.
    Onion Flan   Ingredients required: Eggs, bacon, onion,
    (page 18)   mushrooms (use tinned as substitute),
                  flour, butter, cream (use tinned as substi-
                  tute).

(*e*) *Egg and Bacon*   Time necessary before eating: 40 minutes.
    Pie (page 63)   Ingredients required: Eggs, bacon, cheese,
                  butter, flour, milk.

2. Basically Eggs
(New recipes)

(*a*) *Baked Eggs with*   Time necessary before eating: 10 minutes.
    Cheese   Ingredients required: Eggs, butter, cheese,
                  cream (use tinned as substitute).

Butter individual ramikin dishes, break an egg into each. Sprinkle over grated cheese and seasoning. Pour over each a dessertspoon of cream and bake in a hot oven for about 7 minutes.

(*b*) *Baked Eggs with*   Time necessary before eating: 10 minutes.
    Tomato Ketchup   Ingredients required: Eggs, butter, tomato
                  ketchup, cream (use tinned as substitute).

Butter individual ramikin dishes, break an egg into each. Add about a teaspoon of tomato ketchup. Pour over a dessertspoon of cream. Season and bake in a hot oven for about 7 minutes.

(*c*) *Baked Eggs with*   Time necessary before eating: 10 minutes.
    Shrimps   Ingredients required: Eggs, butter, shrimps
                  or prawns (use tinned as substitute),
                  cream (use tinned as substitute).

Butter individual ramikin dishes. Sprinkle a few shrimps or prawns over the bottom of each dish and break an egg on top. Pour over a dessertspoon of cream, season and bake in a hot oven for about 7 minutes.

(*d*) *Argentine Eggs*   Time necessary before eating: 20 minutes.
                  Ingredients required: Eggs, tin of Mexi-
                  corn or sweetcorn, bacon.

Open a tin of Mexicorn or sweetcorn and heat it. Meantime make some bacon rolls and grill them, then arrange them in a dish around the sweetcorn. Poach sufficient eggs for the number of people being fed, and put them on top of the sweetcorn.

(e) *Eggs Suzette*   Time necessary before eating: 1 hour.
                            Ingredients required: Large size baking-
                            potatoes, butter, cheese, eggs.

Scrub the potatoes, allowing 1 per person, and pierce each potato with a skewer and cook it on it to speed up cooking. This will take about 1 hour in a moderate oven. When the potatoes are baked, cut a hole in the top of each and scrape out the inside into a bowl, and save the skins. Mix the potatoes with plenty of butter, some grated cheese, salt and pepper, then pile the mixture back into the empty skins and keep warm in the oven while you poach one egg per person, which should sit on top of the potato.

(f) *Cheese Eggs*   Time necessary before eating: 15 minutes.
                            Ingredients required: Eggs, butter, flour,
                            cheese, milk.

Hard boil sufficient eggs for the number of people to be fed. Shell them and cut into halves or quarters. Make a thick white sauce to which cheese should be added. Pour it over the eggs in a heatproof dish. Sprinkle on a little more cheese and brown under the grill.

(g) *Curried Eggs*   Time necessary before eating: 30 minutes.
                            Ingredients required: Tin of Le-Ka-Ri
                            mild Malayan curry, eggs, rice.

Hard boil sufficient eggs for the number of people to be fed. Shell them and put them in a heatproof dish. Warm the curry sauce and pour over the eggs. Leave standing in a low oven while the rice cooks. Boil the rice in plenty of salted water. Serve with the rice and as many curry accompaniments as possible (see recipe for prawn curry on page 80).

3. Basically Fish
(Recipes already given)

(a) *Prawn, Cheese and Bacon Flan* (page 19)

Time necessary before eating: 40 minutes. Ingredients required: Prawns, bacon, butter, flour, milk, cheese, sherry, mustard and capers (can be omitted if not available).

(b) *Prawn Delight* (page 31)

Time necessary before eating: 15 minutes. Ingredients required; Prawns, eggs, tomatoes (use tinned as substitute), butter, flour, milk, cheese.

(c) *Rob's Prawns* (page 33)

Time necessary before eating: 25 minutes. Ingredients necessary: Prawns, butter, onion, curry powder, cream (use tinned as substitute) and rice as accompaniment if available.

(d) *Prawn Curry* (page 80)

Time necessary before eating: 15 minutes. Ingredients required: Tin of Le-Ka-Ri mild Malayan curry, prawns, rice.

(e) *Green Pea Prawns* (page 82)

Time necessary before eating: 20 minutes. Ingredients required: Prawns, peas (substitute packet of Surprise peas), butter, flour, milk, sherry.

(f) *Crab Vol-au-Vent* (page 164)

Time necessary before eating: 1 hour. Ingredients required: Crabmeat (substitute tinned), mushrooms (substitute tinned), onion, butter, oil, milk, cream (substitute tinned), eggs, mustard, brandy, flour.

(g) *Tuna Fish Pâté* (page 27)

Time necessary before eating: 15 minutes. Ingredients required: Tuna fish, butter, oil, lemon juice, onion, brandy and toast with which to serve.

(h) *Bacon Queues*   Time necessary before eating: 20 minutes.
    (page 23)   Ingredients required: Bacon, sardines,
                       butter, milk, cheese.

4. Basically Fish
(New recipes)

(a) *Tuna Fish in*   Time necessary before eating: 20 minutes.
    Cheese Sauce   Ingredients required: Tuna fish, butter,
                      flour, milk, cheese.

Make a thick white sauce and when it has boiled for 4 minutes
withdraw the pan from the heat and stir in enough grated cheese
to give it a fairly strong flavour. Break the tuna fish into the
sauce and warm. Season and turn into a greased heatproof dish.
Sprinkle on a little more grated cheese and brown under the grill.

(b) *Tuna Fish and*   Time necessary before eating: 35 minutes.
    Rice Salad   Ingredients required: Tuna fish, rice, eggs,
                      oil, vinegar, onion.

Boil the rice in salt water. When cooked strain and run cold
water through it for several minutes to cool, then drain. Hard boil
the eggs, sufficient for the number of people to be fed, allowing
half an egg per person, and chop. Crumble the tuna fish and grate
the onion into it—about $\frac{1}{2}$ teaspoon per person—mix all the ingredients together and make a French dressing and mix this in
too.

(c) *Crab in Cheese* Time necessary before eating: 20 minutes.
    Sauce   Ingredients required: Crab (substitute
                      tinned), butter, flour, milk, cheese.

Recipe the same as for Tuna Fish in Cheese Sauce, but substitute
crab for tuna fish.

5. Miscellaneous
(Recipes already given)

(a) Tongue and Mushroom Crumble (page 160)

Time necessary before eating: 20 minutes. Ingredients required: Tongue (use tinned as substitute), mushrooms (use tinned as substitute), butter, onion, stock (use cube as substitute), flour, wine if available (if not substitute more stock and a little sherry).

(b) Artichoke Cheese (page 48)

Time necessary before eating: 20 minutes. Ingredients required: Artichoke hearts (use tinned as substitute), butter, flour, milk, cheese and wine if available (if not use more milk and a little sherry as substitute).

6. Miscellaneous
(New recipes)

Dishes using ingredients other than Fish or Eggs for which no recipes have previously been given

(a) Welsh Rarebit

Time necessary before eating: 15 minutes. Ingredients required: Bread, butter, flour, cheese, mustard.

Toast as many rounds of bread as you need to feed your guests, butter and keep warm. Make a very thick and strong cheese sauce, adding the equivalent of $\frac{1}{2}$ teaspoonful made mustard per person to the sauce. Spoon it on to the toast and brown under the grill.

(b) Bacon Potato

Time necessary before eating: 30 minutes. ingredients required: Potatoes or packet of instant, bacon, cheese, butter, milk, cream (use tinned as substitute).

Boil the potatoes—to cook them quickly, after you have peeled them cut them into thin slices. If you are using the instant potato

227

make it up following the directions on the packet. Mash the fresh potatoes when cooked in the ordinary way. Add the cream (about 2 tablespoons per packet or per 6 medium-sized potatoes). Cut the bacon up finely and fry until crisp, then mix with the potatoes and a generous amount of grated cheese. Season carefully. Place the mixture in a flat heatproof dish. Dot with butter and brown under the grill. Serve with a green vegetable or salad if possible, as it is a bit solid on its own.

7. Desserts
(Recipes already given)

(a) *Treacle Tart* (page 171)	Time necessary before eating: 40 minutes. Ingredients required: Golden syrup, butter, flour, lemon juice, white bread from which to make breadcrumbs.
(b) *Zabaglione* (page 202)	Time necessary before eating: 7 minutes, if eaten hot, or 30 minutes if eaten cold. Ingredients required: Eggs, sugar, sherry.
(c) *Chocolate Mousse* (page 195)	Time necessary before eating: 1 hour. Ingredients required: Chocolate, eggs, sugar, brandy.
(d) *Caramelized Fruit* (page 172)	Time necessary before eating: 5 minutes. Ingredients required: Moist brown sugar, any tinned fruit available, but preferably a sharp-flavoured one.
(e) *Fruit Crumble* (page 187)	Time necessary before eating: 40 minutes. Ingredients required: Butter, flour, sugar and any tinned fruit available.

APPENDIX IV

SUGGESTED MONTHLY MENUS

The most difficult thing about entertaining for most people seems to be deciding what to have to eat. To help you with this problem we give below month-by-month suggestions for menus, utilizing foods as they are in season.

January

PRAWN DELIGHT (page 31)
(egg, prawns, cheese)

BACON QUEUES (page 23)
(sardines wrapped in bacon
in a cheese sauce)

PRAWN CHEESE AND BACON
FLAN (page 19)

BLACKBALL BEEF (page 123)
(beef in a sauce with olives and anchovies)
Vegetables: Carrot and sprout casserole,
soufflé potatoes

CLUB BEEF (page 125)
(topside with mushrooms in a wine sauce)
Vegetables: Braised celery, baked potatoes.

CASSEROLED PHEASANT (page 106)
(with water chestnuts, bacon, onion and
red wine)
Vegetables: Courgettes, mashed potatoes
or crisps.

GINGER BRANDY (page 198)
(gingernuts soaked in brandy with
cream)

BANANA CREAM (page 173)
(bananas, cream and brandy)

CARAMELIZED GRAPES (page 175)
(grapes in cream and sherry with
caramel top)

February

SHRIMP PIPPIN (page 36)
(shrimps, apple and celery in a cream sauce)

PORK WITH TOMATOES (p. 119)
(pork chops, mushrooms in a spiced tomato sauce)
Vegetables: Avocado pear and grapefruit salad, noodles.

CHINESE GRAPES (page 175)
(grapes and lychees)

MUSSELS IN MUSTARD SOUP (page 45)

FRICADELLE (page 126)
(minced beef loaf)
Vegetables: Baked tomatoes and onions, potatoes with cheese.

GRAPEFRUIT WITH GIN (page 176)

TURTLE EGGS (page 17)
(eggs in jellied turtle soup)

ARTICHOKE VEAL (page 142)
(fillet veal with artichokes, peppers, aubergines and tomatoes in a cheese and sherry sauce)
Vegetables: Courgettes, mashed potatoes.

APPLE CRUMBLE (page 187)
(apples with crumbly pastry top)

March

PORK PÂTÉ (page 39)
(coarse pâté with pork)

COLMAN'S CRAB VOL-AU-VENT (page 164)
(crab in a mild mustard sauce)
Vegetables: Cucumber and tarragon salad, no potatoes.

PLUM ORANGE CREAM (page 186)
(purée of plums, orange and apples)

PRAWN CHEESE AND BACON FLAN (page 19)

DEVIL'S DELIGHT (page 156)
(kidneys, prunes and apricot brandy)
Vegetables: Tomato and endive salad, rice or noodles.

FRESH LEMON JELLY (page 193)

TUNA FISH PÂTÉ (page 27)

CHIEVELEY CHICKEN (page 86)
(chicken in tomato, herb, wine and cream sauce)
Vegetables: Mixed winter salad, potatoes with cheese.

ORANGE BAKED APPLES (page 179)
(apples baked with slices of orange and honey)

MARINATED PRAWNS (page 32) (prawns marinated with layers of onion)

OLIVE CHICKEN (page 94) (chicken in a port sauce with olives, onions and peppers) Vegetables: Green salad, new potatoes.

EMBALMED MACAROONS (page 199) (macaroons in a rich chocolate sauce)

BACON, MUSHROOM, EGG AND ONION FLAN (page 18)

DIZZY KIDNEYS (page 157) (kidneys in champagne cider) Vegetables: Tossed green salad, noodles.

ORANGE APPLE SNOW (page 178) (purée of orange, apple, egg white and sugar)

CHICKEN LIVER PÂTÉ NO. 2 (page 38)

CRAB CASSEROLE (page 76) (crab with gherkins, red peppers, olives, mushrooms and cheese) Vegetables: Green salad, no potatoes.

ORANGE AND APRICOT CREAM (page 184)

May

SPICY AVOCADO (page 50) (avocado pear mashed up with tomatoes, red, green and chilli peppers)

NO ORDINARY CHICKEN PIE (page 95) (chicken pie with mushrooms, liver pâté, egg and sherry) Vegetables: Courgettes baked with rosemary, no potatoes.

MANDARIN PINEAPPLE (page 177) (fresh pineapple and mandarin orange segments)

CHICKEN LIVER PÂTÉ NO. 1 (page 37)

THREE FISH CASSEROLE (page 79) (crab, prawns, halibut, mushrooms and tomatoes in a sherry sauce) Vegetables: Cucumber salad, new potatoes.

APRICOT ICE CREAM (page 190) (made with fresh apricots)

MUFFLED PRAWNS (page 29) (prawns and cucumber in cheese and mayonnaise sauce)

TONGUE AND MUSHROOM CRUMBLE (page 160) (tongue with mushrooms covered with crisp breadcrumbs) Vegetables: Green salad, new potatoes.

LEMON MOUSSE (page 196)

June

EGG MOUSSE (page 15)
(eggs, consommé and cream)

HAM TRUFFLE (page 21)
(ham, mushrooms and tomato mousse)

RATATOUILLE (page 56)
(onion, garlic, aubergine, peppers, tomatoes and courgettes)

July

CROSSED COURGETTES (page 52)
(courgettes, onion and tomatoes in a cheese sauce)

SMOKED TROUT (page 60)

CRAMMED HAM. (page 20)
(slices of ham stuffed with liver pâté, cream cheese and prunes)

RATATAT VEAL (page 145)
(veal with aubergines, peppers and tomatoes in wine)
Vegetables: Asparagus, noodles.

KIDNEY VOL-AU-VENT (page 161)
(kidneys in a white wine sauce)
Vegetables: Green salad, no potatoes.

COLD SALMON KEDGEREE (page 75)
(salmon, egg, onion and rice)
Vegetables: Mixed summer salad, cucumber salad, no potatoes.

PULLED CHICKEN (page 98)
(cold shredded chicken mixed with egg, bacon, gherkins, onions, potatoes and mayonnaise)
Vegetables: Mixed summer salad, no potatoes.

GLASSHOUSE VEAL (page 144)
(fillet veal with cucumber, pears, mushrooms, peppers, rice and tomatoes)
Vegetables: Fresh garden peas, new potatoes.

PRAWNS WITH TOMATOES AND MUSHROOMS (page 81)
prawns, mushrooms and peppers in a spiced tomato sauce)

FRESH RASPBERRIES AND CREAM

STRAWBERRY MERINGUE LAYER CAKE (page 183)

CHERRIES IN WINE (page 174)
(fresh cherries in red wine and redcurrant jelly with brandied cream)

PEACHES IN WINE (page 180)

ZABAGLIONE (page 202)
(eggs, sherry and sugar)

BLACKCURRANT ICE CREAM (page 190)

September

PORK PÂTÉ (page 39)
(coarse pâté made with liver and pork)

THREE FISH CASSEROLE (page 79)
(crab, prawns, halibut, mushrooms and tomatoes in a sherry sauce)
Vegetables: Courgettes, mashed potatoes.

BLACKBERRY MOUSSE (page 194)

October

BONFIRE MELON (page 30)
(melon with shrimps in a cream curry sauce with cashew nuts)

PRAWN COATED CAULIFLOWER (page 34)
(cauliflower studded with prawns and coated with mayonnaise)

FILLED MUSHROOMS (page 53)
(flat mushrooms stuffed with bacon, breadcrumbs and cheese)

BELTED BEEF (page 122)
(topside, mushrooms, peppers and garlic)
Vegetables: White cabbage, tomatoes and onions casserole, mashed potatoes.

CASSEROLED GROUSE (page 104)
(old grouse casseroled with bacon, button onions, tomatoes and mushrooms in a spiced wine sauce.)
Vegetables: Turnips, potato crisps.

COLONEL'S NOSTALGIA (page 90)
(chicken in a cream and light curry sauce)
Vegetables: Courgettes, mashed potatoes.

CHOCOLATE MOUSSE (page 195)

LEMON SYLLABUB (page 185)
(lemons, cream, sherry and sugar)

CARAMELIZED CITROUS FRUIT (page 172)
(fresh orange and grapefruit segments in liqueur with a caramelized top)

November

SMOKED SPRATS (page 60)

CASSEROLED PIGEON (page 106)
(pigeon casseroled with water chestnuts, bacon, onion and red wine)
Vegetables: Braised celery, soufflé potatoes.

CRÈME BRÛLÉE (page 201)
(very rich baked custard with caramelized top)

November

PINEAPPLE PYRE (page 22)
(pineapple with smoked ham
and cream cheese)

DUNCAN'S SOUP (hot) (page
44)
(combination of vichyssoise,
chicken stock, shrimps,
watercress and spices)

December

PÂTÉ NO. 1 (page 37)
(rich chicken liver pâté)

KIPPER PÂTÉ (page 24)

PRAWN AND CREAM CHEESE
PÂTÉ (page 27)

235

OXTAIL (page 128)
Vegetables: Braised leeks, baked potatoes.

DE LUXE DUCK (page 102)
(duck with orange, almonds and brandy)
Vegetables: Avocado pear and grapefruit
salad, mashed potatoes.

JERUSALEM SCALLOPS (page 78)
(scallops with Jerusalem artichokes in a
cheese sauce)
Vegetables: Mashed potatoes.

ORCHARD CHICKEN (page 91)
(chicken in a cheese sauce with cherries)
Vegetables: Courgettes, mashed potatoes.

KIDNEY BACON PIE (page 155)
(kidneys in a pie with bacon, mushrooms
and tomatoes in a spiced wine sauce)
Vegetables: Baked fennel, mashed potatoes.

TREACLE TART (page 171)

LEMON MERINGUE PIE (page 170)
(flan filled with lemon mixture,
topped with meringue)

PINEAPPLE MEDLEY (page 182)
(fresh pineapple shell filled with
other fresh fruits in white wine)

BRANDY SNAPS (page 169)
(thin ginger biscuits rolled and
filled with cream)

LEMON MOUSSE (page 196)

Note: The various vegetable accompaniments suggested are only a guide to the type of vegetables that go with the
dish, but as so often it is the vegetables that defeat the cook host/hostess, we have tried in as many cases as possible
to use vegetables that can be cooked in the oven, or will not mind being kept waiting. Recipes will be found in
Appendix II (pages 212–20).

INDEX

236